WHOSE GOD IS GOD?

Exploring the Concept of God within Religions

Published by
Adonis & Abbey Publishers Ltd
St James House
13 Kensington Square
London
W8 5HD
Website: http://www.adonis-abbey.com
E-mail Address: editor@adonis-abbey.com

Nigeria:
No. 3, Akanu Ibiam Str.
Asokoro,
P.O. Box 1056, Abuja.
Tel: +234 7066 9977 65/+234 8112 661 609

Year of Publication 2013.

Copyright © Ezenweke, Elizabeth Onyedinma

British Library Cataloguing-in-Publication Data
A catalogue record for this book is available from the British Library

ISBN: 978-1-909112-45-2

The moral right of the author has been asserted

All rights reserved. No part of this book may be reproduced, stored in a retrieval system or transmitted at any time or by any means without the prior permission of the publisher

WHOSE GOD IS GOD?

Exploring the Concept of God within Religions

Edited By

Ezenweke, Elizabeth Onyedinma

Table of Contents

CHAPTER ONE
God, Religion and Man: An Overview
....5

CHAPTER TWO
God within the Parameters of Divine Thanatology and Agnosticism
....17

CHAPTER THREE
The Judeo-Christian God
....29

CHAPTER FOUR
God and Islam
....49

CHAPTER FIve
God and the New Age Movement
....67

CHAPTER SIX
God-Talk in Theistic Perspectives
....87

CHAPTER SEVEN
God in African Traditional Religion
....109

CHAPTER EIGHT
Chi N'eye Ndu: God in an Igbo-African Category
....133

CHAPTER NINE
God is God: A Relationship
....153

Index..160

CHAPTER ONE

God, Religion and Man: An Overview

Ezenweke, Elizabeth Onyedinma

Introduction

The issue of religion and the practice of it has been long standing, producing sameness of points as well as points of departure in almost all of human societies. The term religion has been widely defined and explained in various aspects of life, to the extent that one may boldly state that it has been one of the issues that have received the widest attention in the human world.

Furthermore, it can be said that it is one of those words that has no single acceptable definition. This may be due to the fact that religion or its subject matter is viewed from diverse perspectivesand from a wide range of disciplines: religious studies, sociology, anthropology, theology, philosophy, historical studies and lots more. This has, therefore, created the existence of various shades of definitions and concepts. In fact, the gap is further widened by the elusive nature of the subject matter of religion. That is to say, in an attempt to define religion, one needs to appreciate the indefinable paradox that exists within the core of defining religion because of its elusive nature.Religion as Defined and Explained

Etymologically, religion is derived from the Latin word "religionem" which literally refers to respect for what is sacred or reverence to God or for the gods.[i] For others, religion is often refered to as a collection of cultural and/or belief systems and worldview which establishes symbols that link and connect man to his God or the physical world to the spiritual world and, in addition, determines and reinforces moral values (Geertz, 1993) and as respect for what is sacred, reverence for the gods. (Harper, n.a).

The Oxford English dictionary defines religion as the belief in and worship of a superhuman controlling power, especially a personal

God or godswhile the Webster's Third New International Dictionary defines religion as; the personal commitment to and serving of God or a god with worshipful devotion, conduct in accordance with divine commands especially as found in accepted sacred writings or as declared by authoritative teachers, a way of life recognized as incumbent on true believers and typically the relating of oneself to an organized body of believers, as the body of institutionalized expressions of sacred beliefs, observances and social practices found within a given cultural context, as a personal awareness or conviction of the existence of a supreme being or of supernatural powers or influences controlling one's own, humanity's, or all nature's destiny and as a cause, principle, system of tenets held with ardor, devotion, conscientiousness and faith, a value held to be of supreme importance.

The Oxford English Dictionary defines religion as an action or conduct indicating a belief in, reverence for, and desire to please a divine ruling power; the exercise or practice of rites or observances implying this, a recognition on the part of man of some higher unseen power as having control of his destiny, and as being entitled to obedience, reverence, and worship; the general mental and moral attitude resulting from this belief, with reference to its effect upon the individual or the community; personal or general acceptance of this feeling as a standard of spiritual and practical life.

Scott and Marshall (2005) defined religion as "a set of beliefs, symbols and practices (for example, rituals), which is based on the idea of the sacred and which unites believers into a socio-religious community" (p.560). Iwe (2003) avers that:

> Religion may be considered from four basic points of view namely, subjectively, objectively, morally and institutionally. Subjectively defined, religion is man's natural and innate consciousness of his dependence on a transcendence supra-human being and the consequent natural and spontaneous propensity to render homage and worship to him. From the objective point of view, religion may also be defined as a complex or configuration of doctrines, laws and rituals by which man expresses his loyalty to a transcendent Being-the Absolute-God. It is a descriptive phenomenological definition of religion which denotes a moral-spiritual relationship of the creature with his creator. On the other hand, it is defined morally as a virtue in a person. An enduring quality, a habit which disposes

him who has to pay, steadfastly and well, the debt of honour and worship that he owes to God. Subsequently, religion may be viewed and defined institutionally as possessing its own definite system of beliefs, system of activities and system of values like any other social institution (p.199).

Funk and Wagnalls (2004) describe religion as "a belief binding the spiritual nature of man to a supernatural being as involving a feeling of dependence and responsibility, together with the feelings and practices which naturally flow from such a belief (p.1064).

Capenter and Kant (2000) have defined religion as a "whole group of rites performed in honour of the divine being ---"that is the belief which sets what is essential in all adoration of God in human morality. It is the law in us in so far as it obtains emphasis from a law giver and judge over us" (p.120). Religion, therefore, entails man's show of dependency on some sort of supersensible forces and all it requires to adore, worship and maintain cordial relationship with the being or beings both at personal and congregational spheres, often determined by given ecological lenses. Functional definition of religion emphasizes what religion does to individuals and social groups. In established societies, religion is one of the most important institutional structures of making up the total socio- political system.

Religion has also been defined as a collection of cultural systems, belief systems, and worldviews that establishes symbols that relate humanity to spirituality and, sometimes, to moral values. (Hypography Science Forums in Ezenweke, 2013).

However, it is conclusive that humanity from its earliest history continually searches for God and other cosmic powers to which man depended on. This has hitherto, opened many pathways, each in search of a purer relationship with the super -sensible and supernatural beings. Religion, from any perspective it is viewed, should reflect the mutual horizontal and vertical relationship of man, that is, with his fellow man and with the cosmic forces.

In its simplest sense, religion is a system of orientation that finds meaning in the object of devotion to a higher being, mostly supersensible forces. This same higher being is being worshiped or /and venerated by many cultures only under different philosophies and names.

Chapter one	Ezenweke, Elizabeth Onyedinma, in
	Ezenweke, Elizabeth Onyedinma (Ed.)
	Whose God Is God? Exploring The Concept Of God Within Religions
	London & Abuja, Adonis & Abbey Pulishers

Religion is also often used as the synonym with faith and belief but it is differentiated from faith and belief on the basis of the fact that faith and belief could be private while religion has a public aspect. There are numerous other definitions of religion and a sample of them is as shown below:

Table 1: A list of more definitions of religion

AUTHOR/SOURCE	DEFINITION
American Heritage Dictionary	"Belief in and reverence for a supernatural power recognized as the creator and governor of the universe; A particular integrated system of this expression; the spiritual or emotional attitude of one who recognizes the existence of a superhuman power or powers."
John Ayto: Dictionary of Word Origins	"Latin *religio* originally meant 'obligation, bond.' It was probably derived from the verb *religare* 'tie back, tie tight'. It developed the specialized sense 'bond between human beings and the gods,' and from the 5th century it came to be used for 'monastic life'... 'Religious practices' emerged from this, but the word's standard modern meaning did not develop until as recently as the 16th century."
Immanuel Kant	Recognition of all our duties as divine commands."
Ludwig Feuerbach	"Religion is a dream, in which our own conceptions and emotions appear to us as separate existences, being out of ourselves."
E. B. Tylor	"Belief in spiritual things"
Emile Durkheim	"a unified system of beliefs and practices relative to sacred things, that is to say, things set apart and forbidden -- beliefs and practices which unite into one single moral community called a Church, all those who adhere to them."
Emile Durkheim	"Religion is only the sentiment inspired by the group in its members, but projected outside of the consciousness that experiences them, and objectified."

James G. Frazer	Religion is "a propitiation or conciliation of powers superior to man which are believed to direct and control the course of Nature and of human life."
Alfred North Whitehead	"Religion is what an individual does with his solitariness."
William James	"The very fact that they are so many and so different from one another is enough to prove that the word 'religion' cannot stand for any single principle or essence, but is rather a collective name."
Harriet Martineau	"Religion is the belief in an ever-living God, that is, in a Divine Mind and Will ruling the Universe and holding moral relations with mankind."
Rudolph Otto	"Religion is that which grows out of, and gives expression to, experience of the holy in its various aspects."
John Dewey	"The religious is any activity pursued on behalf of an ideal end against obstacles and in spite of threats of personal loss because of its general and enduring value."
Karl Marx	"Religion is the sigh of the oppressed creature... a protest against real suffering... it is the opium of the people... the illusory sun which revolves around man for as long as he does not evolve around himself."
Paul Tillich	"Religion is the state of being grasped by an ultimate concern, a concern which qualifies all other concerns as preliminary and which itself contains the answer to the question of the meaning of life."
Friedrich Schleiermacher	"The essence of religion consists in the feeling of absolute dependence."
Spiro	"An institution consisting of culturally patterned interaction with culturally postulated superhuman beings."
Bradley	"Religion usually has to do with man's relationship to the unseen world, to the world of

	spirits, demons, and gods. A second element common to all religions is the term salvation. All religions seek to help man find meaning in a universe which all too often appears to be hostile to his interests. The world salvation means, basically, health. It means one is saved from disaster, fear, hunger, and a meaningless life. It means one is saved for hope, love, security, and the fulfillment of purpose."
J. Milton Yinger	"Religion is a system of beliefs and practices by means of which a group of people struggle with the ultimate problem of human life."
Clifford Geertz	"Religion is (1) a system of symbols which acts to (2) establish powerful, persuasive, and long-lasting moods and motivations in [people] by (3) formulating conceptions of a general order of existence and (4) clothing these conceptions with such an aura of factuality that the moods and motivations seem uniquely realistic."
Hick	"Religion constitutes our varied human response to transcendent Reality."
Livingston	"Religion is that system of activities and beliefs directed toward that which is perceived to be of sacred value and transforming power."
Wallace	Religion is "a set of rituals, rationalized by myth, which mobilizes supernatural powers for the purpose of achieving or preventing transformations of state in man or nature."
Cunningham, et al.	"Religion signifies those ways of viewing the world which refer to (1) a notion of sacred reality (2) made manifest in human experience (3) in such a way as to produce long-lasting ways of thinking, feeling, and acting (4) with respect to problems of ordering and understanding existence."
Horton	"An extension of the field of people's social relationships beyond the confines of a purely human society... one in which human beings involved see themselves in a dependent position

Chapter one | Ezenweke, Elizabeth Onyedinma, in
Ezenweke, Elizabeth Onyedinma (Ed.)
Whose God Is God? Exploring The Concept Of God Within Religions
London & Abuja, Adonis & Abbey Pulishers

	vis-a-vis their non-human alters"
R. Forrester Church	Religion is "our human response to being alive and having to die"
Robert Bellah	"...a set of symbolic forms and acts that relate man to the ultimate conditions of his existence."
Schmidt, et al.	"Religions, then, are systems of meaning embodied in a pattern of life, a community of faith, and a worldview that articulate a view of the sacred and of what ultimately matters."

Religion: Origin

There are a number of theories regarding the origin of religion. It is stated that essentially all the world's major religions were founded on the principle that divine beings or forces can promise a level of justice in a supernatural realm that cannot be perceived in this natural one (Esptein, 2010).

It is widely believed that the birth of many world religions stems from the vision of some charismatic prophet(s) or leader(s) who emerged at various times in history. These charismatic humans or superhumans often convincingly inspired the imaginations of men of their time that were seeking for a more comprehensive answer to their problems than they feel is provided by everyday beliefs. The outcome is usually the institutionalization of revitalized movement established and developed by such charismatic individuals and the group of supporters. Thus, the varied and various shades of religious practices, creeds and doctrines. According to Monaghan and Just (2000).

> Charismatic individuals have emerged at many times and places in the world. It seems that the key to long-term success – and many movements come and go with little long-term effect – has relatively little to do with the prophets, who appear with surprising regularity, but more to do with the development of a group of supporters who are able to institutionalize the movement. (p.126).

Religion: Categorized

In recent times, within the 19th and 20th centuries, as the academic disciplne of comparative religion started gathering momentum, some scholars began to divide religion into three main categories; world religions, indigenous religions and new religious movements . In this category, world religions refer to transcultural, international religious bodies and indigenous religions cover smaller culture-specific or nation-specific religious groups while new religious movements, refers to recently developed religious bodies.(Harvey, 2000. Some other scholars share the view of modern academic theory of religion known as social constructionism. This theory propagates that religion is a modern concept that suggests all spiritual practice and worship that follows a model similar to the Abrahamic religions as an orientation system that helps to interpret reality and define human beings, (Vergote, 1997).

Some scholars classify religions as either universal religions that seek worldwide acceptance and actively look for new converts, or ethnic religions that are identified with a particular ethnic group and do not seek converts.(Hinnells, 2005). Others reject the distinction, pointing out that all religious practices, whatever their philosophical origin, are ethnic because they come from a particular culture. (Fitzgerald, 2000; Prentiss, 2003).

Religion: Shared Features

Notwithstanding the difference shades of perspectives of religion as earlier pointed out, most known religions share some basic characteristics. For instance, they all have their various narratives, symbols, traditions and sacred histories, and often myths of existence. These issues give meaning to life and explain the reason and status of life in the universe. They further articulate, form and reinforce the desired laws, moral and ethical dispositions. Monaghan and Just (2000) corroborate that other shared features of religious sets include:

Chapter one | Ezenweke, Elizabeth Onyedinma , in
Ezenweke, Elizabeth Onyedinma (Ed.)
Whose God Is God? Exploring The Concept Of God Within Religions
London & Abuja, Adonis & Abbey Pulishers

a. A generally accepted behavioural pattern.
b. Hierarchical order of clerics/leaders
c. An established process of admitting and categorising membership.
d. Established lay faithful and defined roles of various categories of members.
e. Established place, and pattern of worship
f. Fixed daily or/and weekly hours of worship or meetings.
g. Commemoration of historic events in form of feast, festivals, holidays and abstenance of various forms.
h. The philosophy that knowledge and belief is gained through divinely appointed leaders, sacred texts/scriptures or from revelation.
i. They enable adherents to accommodate anxieties and manage misfortunes by providing sets of answers to how and why things in the world are what and how they are.
j. Other practice such as commemoration of the activities of the Supreme Being or other spiritual forces like the saints in Christianity, sacrifices, festivals, feasts, initiations, funerary services, matrimonial services, meditation, music, art, dance, public service, or other aspects of human culture.

It is important to note that in many cases, the word religion is used interchangeably with faith or belief system, but religion differs from private belief in that it has a public aspect.

God, Religion and Man

If diagrammatically represented, religion is at the center between God and man. In other words, religion is the bridge that connects God and humanity. It is religion that bridges God and humanity. Theories and narratives about, and methods of worship of deities, are to a large extent, a matter of religion and adherents of religion are human beings. In the history of humanity, man worships God through the process of religion. Religion is, therefore, the ontological link between God and humanity.

The Supreme Being in many religions, especially in African traditional religion is believed to be invisible or inaccessible to humans since he is conceived to dwell in remote and holy places such as: heaven, hell, sky, the under-world, under the sea, in the high mountains or deep forests, or in a supernatural plane or celestial sphere. In many, if not all cases, the Supreme Being rarely reveals or manifests Himself to humans, and yet, humans conceive him and feel his presence.

It is not clearly defined whether or not man feels obliged to venerate the Supreme Being out of love for his supremacy or his kindness to man rather than for fear that Supreme Being might withdraw his protection or favour. In any case, it is obvious that man worships the Supreme Being and acknowledges his supremacy and nourishes them with devotion and worship while the Supreme Being displays his sovereignty over humans, punishing and rewarding them, but also dependent on their worship. (Boyer, 2001). The justice of God demands that man is punished as well as appropriately rewarded, if he or she does what is good or bad. That does not undermine that the friendly relationship between the two. (Ezenweke, 2013). As earlier noted, the Supreme Being is conceived to be invisible or inaccessible to humans and yet, they need to interract with him. This has resulted in various shades of interpretations of the Supreme Being as well as many modes of interraction and worship. It is, therefore, recorded that from the earliest available history, the issue of religion and the elements of religion have been one of the major causes of conflicts and wars in different parts of the world. The observed anomaly has far reaching consequences on the conduct of social relations and is having manifold implications on sustainable developments in different parts of the world. Worse still, there is abundant literature that some of the remote causes of religious crises may be matters of semantics. From the knowledge obtained from a long teaching of comparative religious ethics, it may be detected that often times, people destroy themselves and their societies over various versions of the same phenomenon hence, the need to publish a book on the concepts of God amongst world religions. Again, from

Chapter one	Ezenweke, Elizabeth Onyedinma, in
	Ezenweke, Elizabeth Onyedinma (Ed.)
	Whose God Is God? Exploring The Concept Of God Within Religions
	London & Abuja, Adonis & Abbey Pulishers

experience, God seems to mean similar if not the same to Christians, Muslim and African traditional religion. It is arguable to state that the main essence among major religions is often the same while major variations are situated in language, doctrine and mode of worship. The main thrust of the following chapters of this book, therefore, is to cast a look on the concept of God among some major world religions with a view to demonstrating whether or not there is a point of relationship among these religions.

Reference

Boyer, P. (2001). *Religion Explained,.* New York: Basic Books.

Capenter and Kant

Esptein, G. M. (2010). *Good without God: What a Billion Nonreligious People Do Believe.* New York: HarperCollins.

Ezenweke, E. O (2013). Pentecostalism and the Culture of Fear in Contemporary African Communities: A Paradigm Shift. In American International Journal of Contemporary research, Vol. 3. No. 5 may 2013.

Fitzgerald, T. (2000), *the Ideology of Religious Studies.* New York: Oxford University Press

Funk & Wagnalls (2004). *The New International Websters Comprehensive Dictionary of the English Language. Encyclopedic edition.* Florida: Typhooon.

Geertz, C. (1993) *Religion as a Cultural System.* In: The interpretation of Cultures: Selected Essays. USA: Fontana Press.

Harvey, G. (2000). *Indigenous Religions: A Companion.* London and New York: Cassell.

Hinnells, J. R. (2005). *The Routledge Companion to the Study of Religion.* USA: Routledge.

Iwe, N. S. (2003). The Inseparable Social Trinity: Religion, Morality and Law. Calabar: Seas.

Monaghan, J; Just, P. (2000). *Social & Cultural Anthropology.* New York: Oxford University Press.

Prentiss. C. R. (2003). *Religion and the Creation of Race and Ethnicity.* New York: NYU P.

Scott, J, & Marshall, G. (2005). *Oxford Dictionary of Sociology.* New York: Oxford.

The Oxford English Dictionary, (1971). http://atheism.about.com/od/religiondefinition/a/dictionary_old_2.hVergote, A. (1997). Religion, Belief and Unbelief: A Psychological Study. Leuven: University Press.

CHAPTER TWO

God Within the Parameters of DivineThanatology and Agnosticism

Kanu, Ikechukwu Anthony (OSA)

Introduction

A couple of contemporary philosophers have protested the reality of God. These range from outright denials (atheism) via divine thanatology (God is dead) and consequent replacements of God with other items like man, the world and the state, up till more modest views like Russelian agnosticism, which argues that we cannot prove God's existence (Iroegbu, 2002). Added to these are many self-described atheists, who are sceptical of all supernatural beings and cite lack of empirical evidence for the existence of deities or God. Others argue for atheism on philosophical, social or historical grounds (Kanu 2012). Hence, it is in view of this that this chapter is poised to, briefly, expose the arguments of prominent names in the school of thought of atheism, like: Ludwig Feuerbach, Sigmund Freud, Jean Paul Satre, Emile Durkheim, Karl Marx, Bertrand Russell, Friedrich Nietzsche and others, against the existence of God.

Ludwig Feuerbach (1804 – 1872)

According to Harvey (2007), Ludwig Feuerbach, (1804–1872) was born in Landshut, Bavaria into a distinguished family of five sons and three daughters. The father, who dominated the family, was a famous professor of jurisprudence and, a political liberal. As a child Ludwig was very religious, but while attending the Gymnasium in Ansbach he was introduced by his tutor to the speculative Christian theology propounded by the Hegelian theologian Karl Daub at Heidelberg University. Determined to study theology, Feuerbach, with his father's permission, entered Heidelberg in 1823. He was however, troubled by the inability to reconcile his belief in a personal deity with the pure Vernunft of Hegelian philosophy. In the spring of 1824, he went to Berlin where he sat through Hegel's summer semester lectures of 1824 in Logic and Metaphysics and the Philosophy of Religion and this experience, he wrote later, became the turning point of his life.

In his early youth Feuerbach was a fervent believer in God, and had acknowledged that God was his first and foremost thought. However, things took a different turn when he later became convinced that the existence of God could not be proved rationally. He, then, denied the existence of God altogether. The only mission left to him was to prove to believers that God is simply an allusion, a projection of the qualities we find in human nature itself (Perez, 1978). He maintains that God is no other than the projected image of human nature. Man having stripped himself of his best qualities, projects them into an imaginary being called God. Thus, God is an imaginary being formed imaginatively by man through the projection of his best qualities. When man thinks he is worshipping God, he is actually worshipping his own nature since what he calls God is simply his own nature in its perfect form. In reality, therefore, God does not exist. Man is only worshipping himself and praying to himself (Omoregbe, 2000).

Subsequently, he upholds that the statements of religion about God are the illusory dreams of individuals who project their own being into an abstract idea. The real object of religion is the essence of the individual, and human beings are their own God. Hence, the divine is nothing else than the human being, or, rather, human nature purified, freed from the limits of the individual man, made objective – i.e., contemplated and reversed as another, a distinct being (Perez, 1978). In Essence, God does not exist!

*Jean Paul Satre (1905 – 1980)*Jean Paul Satre was the son of Jean-Batiste, a naval officer. According to Thomas (2004), he is arguably the best known philosopher of the twentieth century. His indefatigable pursuit of philosophical reflection, literary creativity

---

| Chapter two | Kanu, Ikechukwu Anthony (OSA), in Ezenweke, Elizabeth Onyedinma (Ed.) *Whose God Is God? Exploring The Concept Of God Within Religions* London & Abuja, Adonis & Abbey Pulishers |

and, in the second half of his life, active political commitment gained him worldwide renown, if not admiration. He is commonly considered the father of Existentialist Philosophy, whose writings set the tone for intellectual life in the decade immediately following the Second World War.

Satre (1951) tries to prove that God does not and cannot exist from three main arguments, namely:

a. Argument from human freedom.
b. Argument from man's subjectivity
c. Argument from the very idea of God itself.

Satre (1951) argues that, if God were to exist and man were subordinate to him, man would not be free. It is either there is no God, and man is not free, or man is free and there is no God. But we know that man is free. Therefore, there is no God. Satre seeks to champion the thinking that:

If God exists, he would annul man's freedom. But since it cannot be denied that man is free, God does not exist. Satre (1951) asserts that, God cannot exist because the freedom that tradition attributes to God actually belongs to human beings. This is due to the fact that, his conception of human freedom leaves no room for God. Freedom is creative, radical, and constitutive. It is absolute because no one and nothing else can snatch it away from us (Perez, 1978). Thus, if God exists, he would be our creator. That would mark the end of human freedom, for then we would have an essence and our whole life would be fixed ahead of time in accordance with some divine pattern.

His second argument is based on man's subjectivity (the inner dimension of man's being: man's interior.) Here, Satre argues that if God were to exist, man would have no subjectivity, for God's penetrating gaze would rob man of his subjectivity. Man's subjectivity would disappear beneath the searching eyes of God. And God's look would be one that could not be countered with a counter look. Man's innermost being would be open to God's eye and the latter would have no secret (Omoregbe, 2000). This is because a divine look (if god were to exist) would be a look that could not be confronted with a counter look. It would penetrate man's subjectivity without resistance and the latter would vanish before it. If then, God were to exist, man would have no subjectivity, but if man has subjectivity, then God does not exist. But we know that man has subjectivity, therefore God does not exist.

Sartre's third argument for the non – existence of God is conceived as *Ens Causa Sui*, that is a being who is the cause of his own being. But this, according to Satre (1969), involves a contradiction. How can a being be the cause of his own being? To be the cause of his own being, such a being would have to exist first, and this is clearly a contradiction. To found its own being, it would have to exist at a distance from itself and that would imply a certain annihilation of the being founded, as of the being which founds. But this is impossible because it involves a contradiction. Therefore, "the *Ens Causa Sui*, which religion calls God" does not and cannot exist. The idea, then, is contradictory.

Sigmund Freud (1856 – 1939)

Sigmund Freud was born May 6, 1856, in a small town, Freiberg, in Moravia. His father was a wool merchant with a keen mind and a good sense of humour. His mother was a lively woman, her husband's second wife and 20 years younger. She was 21 years old when she gave birth to her first son, her darling, Sigmund. Sigmund had two older half-brothers and six younger siblings. When he was four, the family moved to Vienna, where he lived most of his life (Boeree, 2009).

He was a brilliant child, always at the head of his class. He went to medical school, one of the few viable options for a bright Jewish boy in Vienna those days. There, he became involved in research under the direction of a physiology professor named Ernst Brücke. Brücke believed in what was then a popular, if radical, notion, which we now call reductionism. Freud would spend many years trying to "reduce" personality to neurology, a cause he later gave up on (Boeree, 2009).

Chapter two	Kanu, Ikechukwu Anthony (OSA), in Ezenweke, Elizabeth Onyedinma (Ed.) *Whose God Is God? Exploring The Concept Of God Within Religions* London & Abuja, Adonis & Abbey Pulishers

Sigmund Freud also maintains, like Feuerbach, that God is an imaginary being which in reality does not exist. God, according to Freud, is nothing other than an "imaginary father", the "father image" which man formed for himself in his desperate search for security and protection in the face of a hostile world. Led by the "childhood neurosis" of spontaneously turning to its father for protection in times of difficulties, man imagines himself a mighty father ready to help him and give him protection when confronted with the odds of life. But this is an illusion; such a father does not exist outside the human mind (Omoregbe, 2000).

Karl Marx (1818 – 1883)

Karl Heinrich Marx was born May 5, 1818 in Trier, Rhine Province, Prussia in Germany. He was a revolutionary, sociologist, historian, and economist. He published **Manifest der Kommunistischen Partei** (1848), commonly known as *The Communist Manifesto*, the most celebrated pamphlet in the history of the socialist movement. He also was the author of the movement's most important book, *Das Kapital*. These writings and others by Marx and Engels form the basis of the body of thought and belief known as Marxism. He died on March 14, 1883, in London, England.

In the mid 19th century, Karl Marx declared religion to be the "opium of the people" and proposed atheism as the cornerstone of brave new edifice of humanity transformed by total revolution. His was a war cry, in the name of the downtrodden proletariat, against belief in a God who provides for his creatures and on behalf of a new order in which individuals would provide for themselves (Reid, 2003). Since Marx was essentially a revolutionary, his own doctrine is dominated by the idea of praxis. Ideas are legitimate only if they lead to liberative action. And since faith in God must be eradicated if human liberation is to be successful, human beings must be helped to give up their faith in God's existence. Thus, Marxist atheism is not really a philosophic conclusion; instead, it is the speculative justification of a politico – practical decision. Marx proceeds to prove that God has existed as an illusion in people's mind only after he had already decided to do away with God (Perez, 1978). In essence, it could be said that Marx was a humanist, who rejected God in order to liberate people. He never even tried to prove the non – existence of God, he only proposed to put an end to God, to erase any ideas about God from people's minds. For Marx, atheism was a postulate, a cultural presupposition. It is not so much that his philosophy is an atheistic one, rather it presupposes atheism.

Bertrand Russell (1872 – 1970)

Bertrand Arthur William Russell (1872 – 1970) was a British philosopher, logician, essayist and social critic. His most influential contributions include his defence of logicism (the view that mathematics is in some important sense reducible to logic), his refining of the predicate calculus introduced by Gottlob Frege (which still forms the basis of most contemporary logic), his defence of neutral monism (the view that the world consists of just one type of substance that is neither exclusively mental nor exclusively physical), and his theories of definite descriptions and logical atomism. Along with G.E. Moore, Russell is generally recognized as one of the founders of modern analytic philosophy. Along with Kurt Gödel, he is regularly credited with being one of the most important logicians of the twentieth century (Irvine, 1995).

He stands out among the many thinkers who have continued to regard God as an illusion. His philosophy, which seeks to be profoundly humanitarian, is basically Anti – religious (Perez, 1978). This is because he believed that religion was rooted in fear, that it was therefore an evil, from which humanity had to be freed. Searle (1998), records that Russell, being an atheistic philosopher was once asked by a group of Oxford University under-graduates at a dinner meeting what he would say to St. Peter at heaven's gate, if it was true that God exists, having denied his existence all his life. Without much hesitation, he answered, "I would say you did not give us enough evidence" (pp. 36-37).

Chapter two | Kanu, Ikechukwu Anthony (OSA), in
Ezenweke, Elizabeth Onyedinma (Ed.)
Whose God Is God? Exploring The Concept Of God Within Religions
London & Abuja, Adonis & Abbey Pulishers

Bertrand Russell's position as regards God is agnostic. He thereby denies, nor combats the existence of God. Rather, he asserts that the proofs do not convince him and that we are unable to proffer convincing proofs as to this existence. He also maintains that even though we accept the common understanding of God as a supreme personal being, distinct from the world and creator of the world, yet the language deployed in the various proofs does not permit the acclaimed conclusion of God's existence. The arena of God lies outside our limitations. Indeed, the debate concludes -- while we cannot disprove God, we cannot prove him either! (Iroegbu, 2002)

Scientific Atheism

The human search for knowledge rarely alters its direction and mood with radical suddenness; however, there are times when its concerns and emphasis clearly separate it from its immediate past. Such was the case with the dawn of modernism, animated by the Cartesian anthropological philosophy, which threw overboard the theocentricism of the 'Medieval World'. Since then, a kind of infatuation over practical knowledge such as Marxism, Pragmatism, Utilitarianism, has dominated the landscape of the human search for knowledge, giving impetus to science and technology, the conquest of nature (Kanu, 2004). While in the Medieval world, God was seen everywhere in the world, with man abandoning all responsibilities to God, with the advent of science, man is perceived to have come of age and, and thus his own master. Physical science and technology have given man much control over nature. Scientific advancements has or is leading to an absence or even the denial of God. For this reason, man no longer needs God: he can take care of himself. Little wonder then that God is absent from the world as never before. The more science progresses, the less room there seems to be for God. God has become a displaced person (Lutjpen and Koren, 1971).

Chapter two	Kanu, Ikechukwu Anthony (OSA), in Ezenweke, Elizabeth Onyedinma (Ed.) *Whose God Is God? Exploring The Concept Of God Within Religions* London & Abuja, Adonis & Abbey Pulishers

Friedrich Nietzsche (1844 – 1900)

Modern atheism found its major prophet in Friedrich Nietzsche, who was the son of a Lutheran pastor. With an explosive style and an impetuous rush of thought ranging from sacrilege to mysticism, Nietzsche prophetically proclaimed that God was dead, and that human beings had killed him. Unlike Satre who tried to prove the non – existence of God, Nietzsche does not try to prove that God does not exist; he simply tells us that God is dead and he speaks about the death as a dramatic and historical event (Omoregbe, 2000).

The death of God according to Nietzsche means man's liberation. God was an obstacle to man's progress, but now that he is dead, man is liberated. Men should therefore rejoice and take heart, for God the enemy of human development is dead. He refers to the churches, mosques and monuments as his tomb. In Nietzsche's mind, the consequences of the death of God are positive and negative.

Positively, the death of God is a good thing, because God was man's oppressor and enemy of man's progress who impressed the slave morality on man, to deprive man from developing. The slave morality was the means with which God, through the church, was obstructing man's development by stifling his best instincts. On the negative side, however, the death of God is a tragedy for mankind because it has left a vacuum in man's being. It has made human life meaningless and purposeless. The future is bleak and uncertain. Mankind is now empty and drifting aimlessly without light and guidance (Omoregbe, 2000).

According to Perez (1978), one could say that Nietzsche's atheism is really an anti–christian stance rather than atheism in the strict sense. It is a rejection of ethics that champions weakness, simple – mindedness and pettiness. His anti–christian stance is a decision, an act of choice based on personal preference rather than arguments.

Chapter two	Kanu, Ikechukwu Anthony (OSA), in Ezenweke, Elizabeth Onyedinma (Ed.) *Whose God Is God? Exploring The Concept Of God Within Religions* London & Abuja, Adonis & Abbey Pulishers

Other Arguments

Due to the existence of evil, pain, injustice, etc. philosophers argue that; if God exists and we uphold that he is all powerful, all knowing, loving and good at the same time, then, he shouldn't allow evil or pain in a world supposedly created by him. In brief, the problem is that the traditional conception of God implies that if God exists then he knows how to, and is able to, prevent all from suffering. If such a God existed, then we would expect him to prevent all, indeed, from suffering. Suffering though is a familiar part of the world around us, it has not been prevented. Therefore, the argument concludes-- there is no such God.

This is the view of atheists like Albert Camus. He thinks that it is better not to believe in God and do all that is within one's power to fight evil in the world instead of looking up to God for the help that will never come (Omoregbe, 2000). However, theistic philosophers like Saint Augustine have come to prove that God is not and could not be the cause of evil and pain.

Atheists also uphold that if God exists (and wants humankind to know so) he would have brought a situation in which everyone believes in him, but there are unbelievers, so God does not exist. This is similar to the classic argument from evil in that it affirms inconsistency between the world that is, and the world that would be, if God had certain desires combined with the power to see them through.

Finally, according to Bakunin (1916), the idea of God implies the abdication of human reason and justice; it is the most decisive negation of human liberty, and necessarily ends in the enslavement of mankind. He reversed Voltaire's famous aphorism that if God did not exist, it would be necessary to invent him, writing instead that if God really existed, it would be necessary to abolish him.

Evaluation and Conclusion

A cursory glance at arguments from atheists about the non-existence of God reveals a couple of flaws. First of all, it is important to note that neither Feuerbach, Freud, Satre, nor any of the atheists, has been able to prove that God does not exist. An explanation of how the idea of God was formed does not prove that God does not exist, that is, it does not show that there is no being corresponding to such an idea. Thus, such an anthropological or a psychological account of the origin of the idea of God is no proof of His non-existence. . Nor are Satre's arguments valid and convincing. The argument from freedom is invalid because it is based on the assumed incompatibility between God and man's freedom. It is logically possible for God to exist and allow man certain degree of freedom. Therefore, the fact that man is free is no proof of the non-existence of God since the existence of God and man's freedom are not mutually exclusive. In fact, man's freedom is a participation or a derivation from God's freedom.

The argument based on man's subjectivity is even less convincing. A look is not necessarily an attack or an invasion on the person being looked at. For example, a mother's look on her baby, a lover's look on his beloved, cannot be considered as an attack on the other's subjectivity. There is such a thing as a gentle, loving look which is no way an attack on the subjectivity on the person looked at. There is no reason why God's look must be seen as a sword that pierces through man's subjectivity. It could very well be a gentle, loving look like that of a parent on his child.

Satre's third argument is stronger than the first two. Indeed, the term *Ens Causa Sui* (the being that is the cause of his own being) which is traditionally used to describe God is contradictory, and here Satre is right. But it simply means that as a term for describing God it is inaccurate; it does not show that God does not exist. A being cannot be the cause of its own being, as Satre has rightly pointed out. If a being is caused, then it must be caused by something external to it. To say that God is the cause of his own being amounts to saying that he brought himself into existence, and any of these involves a contradiction. For a being has to be in existence already, before it can bring itself into existence, and this is clearly a contradiction. Again, it has to be a being already before it can cause its own being, which is also contradictory, and therefore impossible. It is, therefore, better and more accurate to describe God as the Uncaused Cause of all things rather than as the being who is the cause of his own being (*Ens Causa Sui*). Satre has therefore not proved that God does not exist, he has only pointed out that the term *Ens Causa Sui* used to describe God in classical philosophy involves a contradiction (Omoregbe, 2000). This shows the limitation of human language in defining or describing God.

Further, one could also see in the lives of atheists and nihilists like Satre and Nietzsche, Marx, Engels and Feuerbach, a subdued quest for an absolute, that is, they were all involved in deep reflection for the ultimate and thereby best solution to the problems presented by reality. But, having felt that, reaching that absolute being or good was blocked by the external religious, and socio-political powers of their days, they sought elsewhere in themselves, in man. When Martin Heidegger, disturbingly silent on God, was forced to write, pushed by the Nazi tragic phenomenon, he wrote that "only a God can save us"; and when J.P. Satre at the end of his professed existentialistic – atheistic life, requested for a Catholic Christian funeral, these are proofs of the real theism of their intellectual atheism (Iroegbu, 2002).

The historical turn of events proves that the atheism of these atheists could not hold water. Karl Rahner puts it, "the act of denying God thematically is affirming him unthematically." Internally I argued that there is an embedded theism in their hearts, fighting for the deepest ground of reality: God. Externally, history has proved atheism to be unprovable and thereby unsustainable. None has succeeded in disproving God, nor still eliminating him. On the contrary, the now popular dialogue between ever existing God and diseased Nietzsche (cited by Iroegbu, 2002, p. 60) says: God is Dead. (Nietzsche, 1844 – 1900) Nietzsche is Dead (God, For Ever).

Chapter two	Kanu, Ikechukwu Anthony (OSA), in
	Ezenweke, Elizabeth Onyedinma (Ed.)
	Whose God Is God? Exploring The Concept Of God Within Religions
	London & Abuja, Adonis & Abbey Pulishers

References

Bakunnin, M. (1916). *God and the State.* New York: Mother Earth Publishing Association.

Boeree, G. (2009). *Sigmund Freud.* Retrieved 31st October, 2012 from http://webspace.ship.edu/cgboer/freud.html.

Harvey, A. V. (2007). Ludwig Andreas Feuerbach. Stanford Encyclopedia of Philosophy. Retrieved 31st October, 2012 from http://plato.stanford.edu/entries/ludwig-feuerbach.

Irvine, A. D. (1995). *Bertrand Russell.* Stanford Encyclopedia of Philosophy. Retrieved 31st October, 2012 from http://plato.stanford.edu/entries/russell.

Kanu, I. A. (2012). *The Atheist's Arguments Against the Existence of God.* Lecture note, St Augustine's Major Seminary, Jos.

Luijpen, W. & Koren, H. (1971). *Religion and Atheism.* Pittsburgh: Duquesne University Press.

New York: Basic.

Omoregbe, J. (2000). A Philosophical Look at Religion. Ikeja, Nigeria: Joja Educational Research and Publishers.

Pantaleon, I. (2002). *The Theism of Atheism: Revisiting the Proofs of God's Existence.*

Perez, A. (1978). *Atheism and Liberation.* Mary knoll: Orbis.

Reid, J. P (2003). *Atheism.* New Catholic Encyclopedia. Vol. 1. *Detroit: Gale Group.*

Russel, B. (1979). *The Existence of God.* London: Unwin.

Satre, J. P. (1951). *Le diable est le bon dieu.* Paris: Gallimard.

Satre, J. P. (1969). *Being and Nothingness.* London: Methuen.

Searle, J. (1998). *Mind, Language and Society: Philosophy in the Real World.*

Thomas, F. (2004). *Jean Paul Sartre.* Stanford Encyclopedia of Philosophy. Retrieved 31st October, 2012 from http://plato.stanford.edu/entries/sartre.

WAJOPS. 5. 47

Chapter two	Kanu, Ikechukwu Anthony (OSA), in
	Ezenweke, Elizabeth Onyedinma (Ed.)
	Whose God Is God? Exploring The Concept Of God Within Religions
	London & Abuja, Adonis & Abbey Pulishers

CHAPTER THREE

The Judeo-Christian God

Ogada, Charles. (Rev. Fr.)

Who is God?–A General Prolegomena

Although God is the center of every religion, the concept of God is one of the most difficult subjects in theology or religious studies. This is due to the fact that 'God' is inaccessible to our sensory perception which is the primary tool for human conceptualization. Since mental concepts are dependent on the information gathered through the senses, how could one put into concepts that which itself is beyond the senses? This situation puts religious scholars and experts into real problem immediately they try to define or prove the existence of God. For example, Christian theologians found themselves caught in this enigma. St Thomas Aquinas in his "first cause argument" for the existence of God contradicts the very first premise on which his argument rests – namely that, "Everything that happens has a cause" (Henry, 1997, p 126). If everything that happens has a cause, then what caused God? In the end, Aquinas exempted God from the sway of causality and made him the "first cause" without a cause.

One day, during a homily, the author of this article asked his audience, comprised of more than a thousand people gathered for worship, the gender of God. Is God a man or a woman? This question, as simple as it may seem, threw the gathered community into a conundrum of confusion. There were rumors and murmurs arising from the unconscious indoctrination of religion. Many said, of course, God is definitely a man. One old man raised his hand and pointed to the cross with the images of the crucified Jesus and said, look, he is a man. A minority said that sGod is neither a woman nor a man but that he must be both. A woman braved it and said "God is a woman" to which everyone was sent into a mocking laughter including the one who gave the answer. Then it became clear to all that we do not know the nature of the One whom we had gathered to worship!

To save the situation, we had to fall back to the Catholic Catechism for the definition of God. Most members of the congregation knew this definition by heart: "God is Spirit, who alone exists of himself, he has no beginning or end and he is the creator of all that exists." Then we went further to ask, "If God is a Spirit, what is Spirit?" And the catechism rote definition was given by one old woman in the native language: "Muo bu ihe di adi di ndu, nke n' eweghi ahu, anaghi ahu anya, ma obu nu onu ya, ma obu metu ya aka." Meaning "Spirit is that which exists and is alive, which has no body, cannot be seen, heard or touched" (Catechism of the Christian Doctrine).

The question then arises, if God is a Spirit and a Spirit is that which has no body, how can God be said to be male or female? And if God has no gender, how can we refer to God as "He" or "She" or "It"? (For the purposes of consistency in language and demystification of collective mind set, we shall refer to God as "she" in this work, except in direct quotes). Again, if God is beyond our sensory perception - She cannot be touched, heard, seen or smelt- how can we hope to describe her using sensory categories? The histories of the different religions have battled with this problem of "God definition" over the ages and the Christian religion is not an exception (Hick, 1983, Smart, 1983).

In this chapter, we shall be dealing with this difficult subject and how Christians have tried to come to terms with it. Since God as She is in herself, is not accessible to the physical senses, her reality is always mediated by metaphysical revelations which are always subjective to the one to whom she has revealed herself. In this work, we shall employ the medium of revelations as primary tools for arriving at the concept of God in the Christian religion. Since Christianity is largely an offshoot of Judaism, we shall be concerned with God's Self revelations through the founders of both religion – Moses and Jesus Christ. Consequently, we shall have a historical survey of the development of the concept of God in Christianity,

---

Chapter three	Ogada, Charles. (Rev. Fr.), in
	Ezenweke, Elizabeth Onyedinma (Ed.)
	Whose God Is God? Exploring The Concept Of God Within Religions
	London & Abuja, Adonis & Abbey Pulishers

starting from its roots in Judaism as enunciated in the books of the Old Testament, down to the revelation of God made manifest in the person and deeds of Jesus Christ and how the early Christian community understood this revelation in the New Testament and summarized them in the Christian creedal Formula (regula fidei/veritatis).

We shall try to explore some of the contradictions inherent in the modern Christian understanding of God with a view towards arriving at a clearer image of that which has no image (since God is formless)!

The Christian Concept of God

Old Testament Origins

Man's understanding of God is a historical development and if man understands, it is not God. In many ways, Christianity could be said to be the offshoot of Judaism in scripture, in worship and in faith. Christians believe that the New Testament is the fulfillment of the Old Testament and that Jesus Christ is the concrete manifest and final revelation of the God of the Old Testament, the "Dabar דבר YHWHדבר־יהוה" or "Word of God. The founder of Christianity, Jesus Christ, was a Jew and until his death he practiced the religion of Judaism. In the Gospel according to Mathew, he is reported as saying, "Think not that I came to destroy the law or the prophets: I came not to destroy, but to fulfill" (Matthew 5:17).

The prolog to the Gospel of St John recaptured the myth of origin in the Book of Genesis and demystified this myth in the person and reality of Jesus Christ. In the Old Testament, God created the cosmic universe through her Word and in the New Testament, this Word "becomes flesh" in Jesus Christ. The point here is that John draws an identity between the God of the Old Testament, (YHWH), The Creative Word (Dabar) and reality of Jesus Christ. For John, these three are one. Hence, in the very first verses of the first chapter of his Gospel, he writes:

| Chapter three | Ogada, Charles. (Rev. Fr.), in
Ezenweke, Elizabeth Onyedinma (Ed.)
Whose God Is God? Exploring The Concept Of God Within Religions
London & Abuja, Adonis & Abbey Pulishers |

> In the beginning was the Word (Dabar), and the Word was with God (YHWH), and the Word was God. ... All things were made through him and without him was not anything made that has come into being....And the Word was made flesh (Jesus Christ), and he dwelt among us, full of grace and truth (John 1:1, 3,14).

These verses recaptured the first verses of the first chapter of the Book of Genesis: "In the beginning God created the heavens and the earth....And God said, Let there be light: and there was light...." (Genesis1:1, 3). The identity John made between Jesus Christ, the "Word made flesh" and YHWH was later developed into the Trinitarian doctrine of the Christian faith: That the God of the Old Testament, "YHWH", her Creative Word, Jesus Christ, and her sustaining or preserving energy, the Holy Spirit, are one and the same. If the Christian God is intrinsically linked with the God of the Old Testament, we can only begin to unravel the development of the Christian concept of God if we understand fully the God of the Old Testament.

The Old Testament was not concerned about God's metaphysical nature, although Her actions drew attention to Herself and shed light upon her being (Vaux, 1969). The opening of Genesis reveals God to be the creator of heaven and earth. With Abraham, God began to reveal Herself in a new definitive way. By intervening in Abraham's life, God entered human history (Gn 12:1). She became the God of Abraham, Isaac and Jacob (Ex 6:31) although through the patriarchal period She was known by many names.

The Semites looked upon names as an integral part of the thing named, identical and descriptive of the nature of the name's bearer (Vaux, 1967). As such, by examining some of the important names by which God was known to the Old Testament patriarchs, we may come to understand what idea they had of divinity.

El (Deity)

El is a generic word for god that could be used for any god including Baal, Moloch or Yahweh (El Deity, 2010). The oldest name used for the deity by almost all Semitic people was 'Ēl (written aleph-lamed,

---

Chapter three | Ogada, Charles. (Rev. Fr.), in
Ezenweke, Elizabeth Onyedinma (Ed.)
Whose God Is God? Exploring The Concept Of God Within Religions
London & Abuja, Adonis & Abbey Pulishers

e.g. Hebrew: אל, Arabic: إل or Arabic: الله, cognate to Akkadian: ilu) from the root meaning "strong' (Vaux, 1967; Matthews, 2004). Outside Israel, El was the father of the gods and the Lord of heaven. The noun 'ēl was found at the top of a list of gods as the Ancient of gods or the Father of all gods, in the ruins of the royal archive of the Ebla civilization, in the archaeological site of Tell Mardikh in Syria dated to 2300 BC (Caquot & Sznycer, 1980; van der Toorn, 1999, Schwabe, 1978; Falk, 1996). The form 'ēl appeared in Israelite names from every period including the name Yiśrā'ēl ('Israel'), meaning 'ēl strives' or 'struggled with él'. According to The Oxford Companion to World Mythology",

It seems almost certain that the God of the Jews evolved gradually from the Canaanite El, who was in all likelihood the 'God of Abraham'...If El was the high god of Abraham-Elohim, the prototype of Yahveh-Asherah was his wife, and there are archeological indications that she was perceived as such before she was in effect 'divorced' in the context of emerging Judaism of the seventh century B.C.E. (See 2 Kings 23:15) (Leeming, 2005, p. 118).

In the Old Testament, the name was used with modifiers: She was the everlasting El (Gen 21:33) the Living El (Jos 3:10) and the El of vision (Gen 16:13), El Shaddai (Ex 6:3), El Elyon (Most High God), and Elohim - the often recurring plural form developed from a rare singular Eloah – (Gen 1:1). In the P strand, YHWH says:

"I revealed myself to Abraham, to Isaac, and to Jacob as Ēl Shaddāi, but was not known to them by my name, Yahweh" (Exodus 6:2–3). The identity of Yahweh with either Ēl, in his aspect of Shaddāi, or with a god called Shaddāi is implicated in the Before El's revelation with the name of Yahweh, it is said in Genesis 14:18–20 that Abraham accepted the blessing of El, when Melchizedek, the king of Salem and high priest of its deity El Elyon (Coogan, 2009).

Yahweh's Self Revelation to Moses

God said to Moses in Exodus 3:14-15: "I am that I am"... "This will be my name forever; it has always been my name, and it will be used throughout all generations." Moses represents a turning point in the history and religion of Israel and as such could be said to be the true founder of Israel's religion. A definitive revelation of God in the Old Testament happened in his "burning bush" experience on the mount of Sinai. To him, God revealed his very name: She who was "the God of your fathers, the God of Abraham, Isaac and Jacob" (Ex 3:6) was to be called "Yahweh", "She who is" or "She who is the existence of whatever exists" (Ex 3:14-15): ever present active and powerful in Israel, affecting the liberation of her people from Egypt and freely and graciously entering into a covenant with them.

When Moses asked God for Her name, God replied "I Am That I Am", followed by "I Am", and finally "YHWH": "I Am That I Am [Ehyeh Asher Ehyeh…] Thus shalt thou say unto the children of Israel, I Am hath sent me unto you. [...] YHWH, God of your fathers, [...] this is My name forever" (Exodus 3:13–15).

Yahweh (Hebrew: יהוה), often rendered Jehovah or the LORD (in small capitals), is a modern pronunciation of the name as it appears in Hebrew, where it is written without vowels as יהוה (YHWH), called the Tetragrammaton. The term tetragrammaton is from the Greek τετραγράμματον, meaning "[a word] having four letters"). It is derived from tetra "four" + gramma (gen. grammatos) "letter") (Online Etymology Dictionary, 2005?). Biblical Hebrew was written with consonants only, meaning that the name of God is written YHWH. The original pronunciation of this word was lost many centuries ago, but the available evidence indicates that it was in all likelihood Yahweh (Miller, 2000, p. 2). At some point a taboo on saying the name aloud developed in Judaism, and rather than pronounce the written name, other titles were substituted, including "Lord" (in Hebrew Adonai, in Greek Kyrios).

We might note in passing that YHWH's Self revelation to Moses as "I Am That I Am" is an interesting revelation which may have important links to Hinduism; as were most of the eastern religions. For example, God is referred to as "Aham tat" or "I Am That" in the Amritbindu Upanishad, one of the most ancient scriptures of the Hindu religion (Nisargadatta, 1981, p. 1), dating back before the believed time of the Hebrew exodus from Egypt (1250 BCE)

Chapter three	Ogada, Charles. (Rev. Fr.), in Ezenweke, Elizabeth Onyedinma (Ed.) *Whose God Is God? Exploring The Concept Of God Within Religions* London & Abuja, Adonis & Abbey Pulishers

(http://en.wikipedia.org/wiki/Timeline_of_religion). In one of the verses of this Upanishad, it is written: "That in who reside all beings and who resides in all beings, who are the giver of grace to all, the Supreme Soul of the universe, the limitless being--I am that".

Important Implications of Yahweh's Self Revelation

"Oneness is that to which nothing can be added" – Meister Eckhart.

The name YHWH is a verb form derived from the Biblical Hebrew triconsonantal root היה (h-y-y) "to be" (Brown & Driver & Briggs, 1907, p. 217). YHWH essentially means "beingness", "pure existence", or "I Amness". Pure existence means undifferentiated existence. YHWH could therefore be said "to be" the "isness" of everything that is; the "beingness" in everything that has being, and the existence of everything that exists. Everything that says "I Am" could be said to derive its "I Amness" from YHWH's "I Am" and it is not possible to conceive of a spatial or ontological separation between the two (Ogada, 2011). That a thing exists means that it exists in YHWH. In other words, nothing can exist outside existence. Because YHWH is the presence in all that is present, She is omnipresent, and because she is the consciousness in everything that is conscious, She is all knowing. Nothing can be hidden from YHWH's awareness since every cognitive process invariably has its roots in the 'I Am' concept. Again, YHWH'S omnipotence is derived from the fact that no activity is possible without the "I Am" consciousness. YHWH is the infinite possibility of all potentiality.

In the history of Jewish religion, there was a gradual and progressive understanding of the meaning and implications of YHWH's Self revelation to Moses as "I Am" or "I Am That I AM", and it was only in the person and life of Jesus Christ that this meaning was fully developed.

Israel's concept of God moved from polytheism (worship of many gods) to exclusive monotheism (YHWH as superior to other gods) and universal monotheism (YHWH as the one true God) (Obiorah, 2010). Israel first lived the stage of recognition of the existence of gods. For example, Jacob instructed his household to put away the foreign gods that were with them before presenting themselves to YHWH who appeared to him (Exodus 35,2). In Joshua 24, 14-15, Joshua, the new leader and direct successor of Moses, enjoined on his people to distance from the gods that their ancestors worshiped before they entered the Promised Land.

Scholars argue that Israel inherited polytheism from late first-millennium Canaan, and Canaanite religion. Evidence of Israelites worship of Canaanite gods appears both in the Bible and the archaeological record. For example, references to the Canaanite gods, Resheph and Deber, appear without criticism in the original Jewish text of Habakkuk 3:5. While traditionally these words have been understood to be either Jewish words whose meaning has been derived from characteristics of these Canaanite deities (Botterweck, Ringgren & Fabry, n.d.) or references to demons (van der Toorn, 1999) some interpret these as evidence of Israelites recognition of these gods as part of the military retinue of Yahweh (Smith, 2001, p. 67-68).

Secondly, YHWH was seen as the exclusive God of the Israelites and superior to other gods. YHWH would not share Her sovereignty over Her people with other gods. She is a jealous God and Her claim over her people was reserve to her alone. Hence, worship of other gods as we read at the beginning of the two versions of the Ten Commandments was forbidden: "You shall have no other gods before me" (Exodus 20,3 cf Deut 5:7, Exodus 34,14).

By the post-xilic period, universal monotheism had emerged: Yahweh was the sole god, not just of Israel, but of the whole world. According to this new stage of understanding, the purported gods of other nations are not gods (cf Jer 2, 11; 10,7). Yahweh is the only true God; other alleged gods are idols, mere works of human hands; they have mouths but do not speak; eyes but do not see. They have ears, but do not hear, noses but do not smell. They have hands but do not feel; feet but do not walk; they make no sound in their throats" (Psalm 115, 5-7). According to Vaux (1967), the full significance of YHWH's name was not immediately understood in this period, but a great advance had been made, for if YHWH existed, other gods did not.

Chapter three	Ogada, Charles. (Rev. Fr.), in
	Ezenweke, Elizabeth Onyedinma (Ed.)
	Whose God Is God? Exploring The Concept Of God Within Religions
	London & Abuja, Adonis & Abbey Pulishers

This universal monotheism was expressly spelt out in Deut 6: 4-9 which contains the great commandment to Love YHWH. "Hear, O Israel: The LORD our God, the LORD is One. And thou shall love the LORD thy God with all thy heart, with all thy soul, and with all thy strength." For Duane (2001), the Hebrew Bible puts emphasis on this text of Deut 6:4 by enlarging two letters in its sentence that contains just six words, so as to call the attention of readers on the passage. This later became the Shema which every Jew recites twice daily. It is called Shema because it begins with the Hebrew imperative masculine singular, Shema (Obiorah, 2011).

In his prayer of the dedication of the temple, King Solomon entreated the Lord to hear his petition "so that all the people of the earth may know that the Lord is God; there is no other" (1Kings 8: 60). Hezekiah's prayer includes similar monotheistic formula: "You are God, you alone" (2 Kings 19:15). In Deut 4:35, Moses reminds the people: "To you it was shown so that you would acknowledge that the Lord is God; there is no other besides him". In Isaiah (Isa 40 -55) which was addressed to the Jewish exiles in Babylon, there are frequent reference to the non-existence of alleged gods. There is no other god besides the true God. (cf: Isa 41, 29; 43,10; 44,8; 45, 4-6, 14-21; 46,9).

However, a burning question that is pertinent to the foregoing is: Why do the Ten Commandments declare that there should be no other gods "before Me" (YHWH), if there are no other gods at all? The author of this article feels that the essence and meaning of YHWH's name is to be found in the resolution of this puzzle. To release this, let us look at three possible understandings of this fundamental revelation expressed so powerfully in the first and most important Commandment of the Bible: "Listen Oh Israel, God is One and only. You shall not worship any other God apart from Yahweh".

a) YHWH as One Among Many

The first understanding is to interpret the Hebrew numerical masculine singular ehad which generally means "one" as "unique". For Obiorah (2009, p. 136), "the text does not say that YHWH is the only God, rather it only affirms the uniqueness, singleness of the name". Hence, Obiorah maintains that this word "ehad" used in Deuteronomy does not exclude the existence of other gods, but is concerned with the "oneness of YHWH, oneness of cult, and oneness of place of worship – the Temple in Jerusalem".

However, the oneness of YWHH cannot be divorced from the meaning and very nature of YHWH. If YHWH is Who YHWH has revealed itself to be, namely, "Pure Existence", (the term "I Am That I Am" or "Ehyeh Asher Ehyeh" is best understood as "being" or "existence" without qualification or differentiation) it is impossible to think of any other god existing outside YHWH. If YHWH is pure existence, (that is, undifferentiated existence) it means that YHWH is the existence of all that exists (that is, differentiated existence). If YHWH is the I Am That I Am (that is, undifferentiated I Am), it means that YHWH is the "I Am" of all that is (that is, differentiated I Am or "I Am this or that" particular thing). Therefore, if YHWH is the existence of all that exists, the I Am of all that says I Am, it logically follows that what we term as "other gods" are indeed "YHWH". If a god possesses the attribute of existence, this existence is itself YHWH. Consequently, no god can exist apart from YHWH just as we cannot conceive of any existence outside existence.

The enigma we must resolve here is why the commandment prohibits the worship of other gods if indeed there are no other gods at all. We might begin to see the missing piece in the puzzle when we reckon that the Bible consistently states that these "other gods" are false – that is – they don't exist. Consequently, when one thinks that there are other gods apart from YHWH, one creates false gods. These gods are false because they are imaginary creation of the mind. "They have mouths but do not speak; eyes but do not see. They have ears, but do not hear; noses but do not smell. They have hands but do not feel; feet but do not walk; they make no sound in their throats". (Psalm115, 5-7). The worship of other gods means indulging in the illusion that there are other gods when truly there are none. This illusion is associated with imaginary (mental) creation and is the reason why the second commandment forbids images of YHWH.

Chapter three	Ogada, Charles. (Rev. Fr.), in
	Ezenweke, Elizabeth Onyedinma (Ed.)
	Whose God Is God? Exploring The Concept Of God Within Religions
	London & Abuja, Adonis & Abbey Pulishers

Images are false creation of reality. Even though they resemble reality, they lack reality. Ogada (2011) is of the view that the mind creates images of the (YHWH) and makes you think that the image is the reality. Ogada (2011) makes an analogy with the image of a mother:

> The beautiful picture of your mother reminds you of her whenever you look at it. This image also evokes a feeling of love and longing in your heart to be with your real mother. However, no matter how much you cherish and adore this picture, it can never give you the experience of your living mother. To confuse the reality of your mother with her image is the idolatry, which this (second) commandment wants to eliminate (p. 41).

We may note here that there is no ontological difference between the picture of the mother and the living mother. That is, the image has no existence without the reality. The Reality is pure existence, while the image is derived existence. Even this image which the mind makes of Reality (YHWH) is distorted because the mind sees in fragments and cannot perceive Reality as a whole. Like the analogy of the seven blind men's description of the elephant, the combination of the fragmentary images of the mind cannot give the picture of the whole. Most importantly, a picture of Reality (YHWH) can only be made if one is separate or different from Reality. If, however, one is not separate from YHWH, where is the second to take a picture? Logically, an omnipresent YHWH cannot have an image. An infinite force that is everywhere at once, is obviously without a specific form.

b) YHWH as One but Separate

The second possible understanding is to conceive of YHWH as one and only, but still separated from her creation. In the Old Testament understanding, YHWH was wholly "other" and separate from all of creation. This was the reason why the Christian idea of "God man" was abhorrent to Judaism. It was unthinkable to conceive of YHWH becoming man, as the gospel of John had it - "and the Word was made flesh". Christianity tried to bridge the gap between YHWH and man but still retained elements of Jewish understanding by maintaining that YHWH became incarnate only in Jesus Christ and not in others.

Chapter three	Ogada, Charles. (Rev. Fr.), in Ezenweke, Elizabeth Onyedinma (Ed.) *Whose God Is God? Exploring The Concept Of God Within Religions* London & Abuja, Adonis & Abbey Pulishers

We can readily see the contradiction inherent in this separation imposed between YHWH and her creation by the two sister religions. If YHWH is pure existence, then creation, in so far as it truly exists, cannot be separated from the existence of YHWH. For example, when we attribute "omnipresence" (equally present everywhere and at the same time) to the nature of YHWH, this contradiction becomes more evident. If YHWH is omnipresent, how can there be a presence outside YHWH? And if every presence is YHWH's presence, how can one be separate from YHWH? According to Ogada (2011, p. 113),

> God's omnipresence means that God alone is. He is the presence of all that is present and he is fully present in his omnipresence. That is, God's presence is continuous, full and integrated. God is not more present in some places, planes or things than he is in others. For example, God is not more present in heaven than he is on earth. Hence, if God is fully above as he is below, then he is continuously full in His omnipresence – in heaven as on earth, in man as in beast, within as without. God is the fullness and what you see as creation is the fullness taken from God's fullness which is the same undivided fullness. There is nothing outside God.

c) YHWH Alone Exists

We take our third understanding from Meister Eckahart's (1994) definition of "One" as "that to which nothing has been added" (p. 182). If nothing can be added or subtracted from the ones of YHWH, it means that YHWH alone exists. YHWH is pure existence. In this understanding, nothing can exist except in the existence of YHWH. YHWH is the "beingness" or "I Amness" of a thing. There is nothing that says "I Am" which does not derive its "I Amness" from YHWH's "I Am". YHWH is the same Self or Consciousness that animates everything. This new understanding was fully developed in the New Testament in the life and teachings of Jesus Christ who fully identified himself with YHWH and revealed the unity of YHWH with all that is.

Jesus' Christological Identification with YHWH

"Truly truly I say to you, before Abraham was born I Am"
- John 8:58

Chapter three	Ogada, Charles. (Rev. Fr.), in
	Ezenweke, Elizabeth Onyedinma (Ed.)
	Whose God Is God? Exploring The Concept Of God Within Religions
	London & Abuja, Adonis & Abbey Pulishers

One of the greatest shocks to the religious authorities of Judaism in the time of Jesus was Jesus' Christological identification with YHWH. Initially, Jesus claimed to be the messenger of YHWH, saying that he has been sent specially into the world by YHWH herself (Mt 10:40; Mk 9:37; Jn 4:34; 5:30; 6:38; 7:29). Secondly, he started claiming special intimacy with YHWH as his Father; the Son of YHWH (Jn 5:25, 9:35; 11:4). Finally, Jesus claimed to be equal to the Father. "The Father and I are one" (John 10:30).

Once Jesus said to his disciples, "If you had known me, you should have known my Father also: and from henceforth you know him and have seen him." To this Philip said to Jesus, 'Lord show us the Father, and it is sufficient for us" and Jesus replied:

"Have I been so long with you, yet you still not known me, Philip? He that has seen me has seen the Father; therefore, how do you say, "Show us the Father"... "Believe me that I am in the Father and the Father in me: or else believe me for the very works' sake" (John 14:7-9,11).

A logical inference we could draw from the above statements of Jesus is his identity with the Father (YHWH). However, one may wonder what Jesus meant by "me" when he remarked "He that has seen me has seen the Father"? Was he refereeing to his physical body? This would have been a contradiction in Jesus' definition of the Father (YHWH) as Pure Spirit: "YHWH is Spirit and those who worship him worship in Spirit and in Truth" (John 4:24). We must, therefore, conclude that the "sight" Jesus was talking about in this passage was a spiritual insight that made one aware of the "I Am" not just in the physical form of Jesus, but in every form. Furthermore, when Jesus said, "whatever you do to any of these, you do it to me", the "me" Jesus was referring to in this statement was definitely not his physical body but to the indwelling "I Am" living in all beings.

In his teachings and actions, Jesus continued to reveal his identity with YHWH and therefore with all that exists. In another passage detailing an argument which ensued between Jesus and some Jews, Jesus was reported to have said to them: "Before Abraham ever was, I Am" (John 8:58). This statement would have been grammatically and existentially incorrect if Jesus was to his physical body which was not up to fifty years according to the reckoning of those to whom this statement was addressed. (John 8:57). Otherwise, Jesus would have said, "Before Abraham ever was, I was" which means he was born before Abraham. Hence, the "I Am" here could not have been the physical body of Jesus. Rather, from all likelihood, Jesus was making a statement of identification with existence itself. In other words, Jesus was likely saying, "Before Abraham ever was, I Am YHWH" or "I Am the very existence of Abraham".

These claims of Jesus infuriated the religious authorities of his time and became the primary accusations that were brought against him during his trial and condemnation by crucifixion before Pontius Pilate. For the Jews, Jesus' identification with YHWH was blasphemous and punishable only by death: "The Jews answered him (Pontius Pilate), 'We have a law, and by our law he ought to die, because he made himself the Son of God'" (John 19:7).

The understanding of YHWH by the Jewish religious authorities (the Scribes, the Pharisees and the Sadducees) during the time of Jesus, as we saw above, was that "YHWH is One but separate". Hence, no one could claim to be equal to him. Within this framework of understanding one could begin to appreciate the predicament of the authorities with regards to Jesus' claims. The sacredness and sanctity of the Name "YHWH" was so removed that this Name could not be uttered. In the Mishna, the utterance of the name was vehemently denounced in rabbinical Judaism: "He who pronounces the Name with its own letters has no part in the world to come!" (M. Sanhedrin, n.d.).

Such was the prohibition of pronouncing the Name as written that it was sometimes called the "Ineffable", "Unutterable" or "Distinctive Name" (Rösel, 2007; Weiss & Soloveitchik 2005; Rozen, 1992). Hence, in the Jewish Law (Halakha) the Tetragrammaton was conventionally substituted by Adonai ("My Lord") when reading the text of the Bible or with "ha- Shem" ("the Name") in everyday speech ("Merriam-Webster's," 2010). The name "Adonai" too was regarded as a holy name, and was only to be pronounced in prayer (Maimonides, Chap.

14:10; Kiddushin, 71a). The Maimonides relates that only the priests in Temple in Jerusalem pronounced the Tetragrammaton, when they recited the Priestly Blessing over the people daily (Maimonides, Chap. 14). Since the destruction of Second Temple of Jerusalem in 70 CE, the Tetragrammaton was no longer pronounced.

We may note here that in 2008, the *"Vatican Congregation for Divine Worship and the Discipline of the Sacraments"* prohibited the liturgical use of Yahweh and directed that the word "Lord" be used instead of Yahweh in English-language worship, and that the local equivalent to the Latin dominus (Lord, Master) be used in all vernacular worship) ("CNS STORY," 2009). This was based on the understanding that Jews at the time of Christ and also early Christians substituted other words rather than pronounce the name (Graham, 2010, p. 51).

If the vocalization of the Name was such a taboo during the time of Jesus, one could only begin to imagine the intensity of the religious shock the Jewish authorities had when Jesus claimed to be that formless YHWH. This explains why they tried with every means available to them to stop him from spreading the "false" doctrine. Even after they had killed him by crucifixion, they tried to stop his followers from spreading his message. In the Acts of the Apostles, it is recorded of Saul who later became Paul:

> And Saul, yet breathing out threatenings and slaughter against the disciples of the Lord, went unto the high priest, and desired of him letters to Damascus to the synagogues, that if he found any of this way, whether they were men or women, he might bring them bound unto Jerusalem (Acts 9, 1-2).

The Early Christian Community Formulation of Faith

"Credo in unum deum" - Regula Fidei.

Jesus' Christological Identification with YHWH marked the point of divergence between Judaism and Christianity. This identity formed the basis of the Trinitarian doctrine of the early Christian faith which became the selfexpression of the early followers of Jesus and was coded in fragments in the New Testament baptismal formulae such as in Mathew 28:19 ("Go ye therefore, and teach all nations, baptizing them in the name of the Father, and of the Son, and of the Holy

Ghost"). The Trinitarian formula was articulated in what was later referred to as "Rule of Faith". Walter (1989) defines "Rule of Faith" as "a concise normative summary of the entire faith which the church has received from the apostles" (p. 251).

For the early Christians, Jesus was the fulfillment of their Scriptures and the Old Testament believe in YHWH, the One and Only, is affirmed and maintained in their faith in Jesus as the LORD. We would note here that prior to this point, the word "Adonai" or "My Lord" is exclusive to YHWH whose Name cannot be uttered. Hence, this Christological affirmation, "Jesus is Lord" (Cf. Acts 1:21; 2:36; 3:20; 4:33; 7:59; Rom 1:4; Phil. 2:11, etc.) originated from Jesus' Selfidentification with YHWH and formed the basis of an individual's membership in the community. The confirmation of faith, "Jesus is Lord" was gradually lengthened to a standard baptismal formula: "In the Name of the Father, and of the Son and of the Holy Spirit" (Walker, 1997, p.72).

It is noteworthy that this formula uses the singular "Name" Onoma instead of "names" onomata. Initiation into the Christian community was conferred not "in the names…" but "in the name…" reflecting the faith of the early Christians in the unity of the Father, the Son and the Holy Spirit (Obiorah, 2009, p. 133). It was an affirmation of their faith in One God but with new insight gained from the revelation of God made in and through Jesus and their personal experiences of him.

From this ancient rite of initiation, there developed the fundamental community self-understanding articulated in the kanon called "Rule of Faith", "Rule of Truth", "Ecclesiastical Rule", "Tradition" or "Kergma" (Walker, 1997, p. 72). A version of this "Rule of Faith" (Regula Fidei) is found in the work of Irenaues, Bishop of Lyon (135-200):

"The Church, though dispersed throughout the whole world even to the ends of the earth, has received from the apostles and their disciples this faith: [she believes] in One God, the Father Almighty, maker of heaven and earth…; and in One Christ Jesus, the Son of God, who became incarnate for our salvation; and in the Holy Spirit, who proclaimed through the prophets the dispensations of God..." (Adversus Haereses, I, 10, 1).

This is the expanded form of the baptismal confession in God the Father, the Son and the Holy Spirit. Both the Apostles' Creed and the Nicene Constantinople Creed have remarkable resemblance to this with regards to their Trinitarian framework. The opening of all forms of Christian creedal formula invariably start with the affirmation "I believe in One God", - "Credo in unum deum".

From the above, we could see that the concept of God had undergone a historical development through the Old Testament down to the New Testament times. The Jews of the Old Testament moved through a long difficult process of understanding of "YWHH as One among many" (where YWHW was conceived as unique among other equally existing gods), to an understanding of "YHWH as One but separate". Here, other "gods" were considered non-existent. However, YWHW was conceived as wholly separate and removed from creation so much so that her Name could not be uttered. This was notwithstanding YHWH's intervention in the course of Israel's history especially in their experiences of deliverance from captivity in Egypt.

In the New Testament, this separation between YHWH and the people (others) was bridged by Jesus, who became the incarnation of the "Word of YHWH" (Dabar YHWH). Hence, the early Christians saw Jesus to be identical with YHWH and in the reality of Jesus, the wholly transcendental unreachable and unutterable YHWH now became immanent and within the reach of all. Jesus became Emmanuel, "God with us" (Matthew 1: 23).

However, this early Christian's expansion in the understanding of YHWH was still influenced by their Old Testament origins. The "separation" imposed between YHWH and others in the Old Testament, was carried over in the New Testament by the separation imposed between Jesus and others. Hence, Jesus became the "Only begotten Son of God" (John 1:18, 3:18, 1 John 4:9) and the "Only One who had seen YHWH" (John 1:18).

In summary, Jesus brought a whole new understanding to the concept of YHWH through his teachings and his lived example. It is important to note that Jesus could not have taught that only him was identical with YHWH. Rather, his Christological identification with YHWH presupposes his identification with everything that has existence. Thus, he taught all to call YHWH, "Our Father" since the "I Am" is the "father" of all existence.

When the Jewish religious authorities accused him of making himself equal to YHWH, he reminded them that their scriptures say that they too are gods and "the scriptures cannot be false" (cf. John 10:36, Psalms 82:6). It is not hard to perceive the straightforwardness of Jesus logic of Oneness: If YHWH Alone exists; it either means that "I Am God" or that "I do not exist". But I do exist since I cannot say "I do not exist", unless "I exist". If I truly do exist, this existence therefore is YHWH. Much of the teachings of Jesus could be seen to revolve round this pivotal axis of meaning: YHWH Alone exists.

From the foregoing, we could reasonable draw the conclusion that the concept of the old testament God centers on these words: "Hear O Israel, the Lord our God is One. There is no other."

Referencess

Brown, F., Driver, S. R. & Briggs, C. (1907). The New Brown–Driver–Briggs-Gesenius Hebrew and English Lexicon.

Caquot, A., Sznycer, M. (1980). *Ugaritic Religion*. Iconography of Religions in Mesopotamia and the Near East. Netherlands: Brill.

Coogan, M. D. (2009). *A Brief Introduction to the Old Testament*. New York: Oxford University Press.

CNS STORY: No 'Yahweh' in songs, prayers at Catholic Masses, Vatican Rules". (2009). Retrieved from
http://www.catholicnew.com/data/stories/cns/0804119.htm.

Duane, L. C. (2001). *Deuteronomy 1, 1-21, 9. In* Word Biblical Commentary *(Vol. 6a.)*. Nashville: Thomas Nelson Publishers.

Eckhart, M. (1994). Meister Eckhart, Selected Writings. *(Davis, O. Trans.)*. London: penguin books.

Chapter three	Ogada, Charles. (Rev. Fr.), in Ezenweke, Elizabeth Onyedinma (Ed.) *Whose God Is God? Exploring The Concept Of God Within Religions* London & Abuja, Adonis & Abbey Pulishers

El Deity. (2010). *Retreived from: http://en.wikipedia.org/wiki/El_(deity)*
Falk, A. (1996). *A Psychoanalytic History of the Jews.* Cranbury, NJ: Associated University Presses.
Fox M. (1983). *Meditations with Meister Echart.* New Mexico: Bear and Company.
Henry, M. (1997). *On not Understanding God.* Dublin: Columbu.
Hick, J. (1983). *Philosophy of Religion.* N. J: Eaglewood cliffs.
Judaism 101 on the Name of God. Retrieved from: jewfaq.org.
Leeming, D. (2005). *The Oxford Companion to World Mythology.* New York: Oxford University Press.
Matthews, V. H. (2004). *Judges and Ruth. In* New Cambridge Bible Commentary. Cambridge: Cambridge University Press.
Meindert D. (2001). *El the God of Israel, Israel the People of YHWH: On the Origins of Ancient Israelite Yahwism. In* Bob B. (Ed.), Only One God? Monotheism in Ancient Israel and the Veneration of the Goddess Asherah. Sheffield Academic Press.
Meindert D. (2001). I have Blessed you by Yahweh of Samaria and his Asherah: Texts with Religious Elements from the Soil Archive of Ancient Israel. *In* Bob B. (Ed.), *Only One God? Monotheism in Ancient Israel and the Veneration of the Goddess Asherah.* Sheffield Academic.
Miller, P. D. (2000). The Religion of Ancient Israel. Westminster: John Knox.
Mishneh Torah Maimonides, Laws of Prayer and Priestly Blessings. Retrieved from http://www.chabad.org/dailystudy/rambam.asp?t Date=3/28/2012&rambamChapters=3
Obiorah, J. M. (2010). *The Bibilical Foundations of Christian Monotheism, in.* B. U. Ukwuije, (Ed.) In God, Bible and African Traditional Religion - *Acts of SIST International Missiological Symposium.* Enugu: SNAAP.
Ogada, C. (2011). The I Am Principle, the Christ Within. *United Kingdom: O Books.*
Rendon, G. (1985). *Religion in the Age of Romanticism.* Cambidge.
Ringgren, G., Fabry, H. (Eds.) (n.d.). *Theological Dictionary of the Old Testament. (Vol. 14.*

Robert K. G. (1997). *No Other Gods: Emergent Monotheism in Israel.* Sheffield Academic Press.

Schleimacher, S. (1958). *On Religion: Speeches to its Cultured Despisers.* New York: Oman

Schwabe, C. W. (1978). Cattle, Priests, and Progress in Medicine. Minneapolis, MN: University of Minnesota Press.

Smith, M. (2001). Untold Stories: The Bible and Ugaritic Studies in the Twentieth Century. Hendrickson Publishers.

Smith, M., Miller, P. D. (1990). *The Early History of God: Yahweh and the Other Deities in Ancient Israel.* Harper & Row.

Smith, M. (2001). The Origins of Biblical Monotheism: Israel's Polythesistic Background and the Ugaritic Texts. Oxford: Oxford University Press.

The Catechism of the Catholic Church Compendium, (2006). Kenya: Kolbe press.

Van der Toorn, K., Becking, B., van der Horst, W. (1999). *Dictionary of Deities and Demons in the Bible.* Retrieved from http://books.google.com/?id=yCkRz5pfxz0C&printsec=frontcover.

Van der Toorn, K. (ed.), (1999). Dictionary of Deities and Demons in the Bible. (2nd ed.), Eerdmans.

Vaux, R. (1967). *The Religion of the O.T. In R. Tricot (Ed.),* New Catholic Encyclopedia (Vol. 6, Part 2, pp. 393-422). Washington D.C: Catholic Univsersity of America.

Williston, W. (1997). *A History of the Christian Church.* Edinburgh: T&T. Clark.

Walter, K. (1989). *The God of Jesus Christ.* New York: Crossroad

CHAPTER FOUR

God and Islam

Faleemu T. M. & Abdu-Raheem M. A.

Introduction

Islam is based on five fundamental principles. The first and the most important of them is *Kalimatu'sh-Shahādah* (Word of Testimony). It is to testify that there is no deity worthy of worship except Allah and that Muhammad is His Messenger. This forms the bedrock of Islamic theology. The remaining four pillars are *Ṣalāt* (daily canonical prayers), *Zakāt* (alms giving), *Ṣawm* (fasting in the month of Ramaḍān) and *Ḥajj* (holy pilgrimage to Makkah). They will be accepted as ᶜ*Ibādah* (acts of worship) and be rewarded only if the first one has been established. Ibn ᶜAbbās is reported to have said:

> A Bedouin once came to the Messenger of Allah and said: "O Allah's Messenger! Teach me the most unusual of knowledge." The Prophet responded, "What have you done with the peak of knowledge so that you now ask about its most unusual things?" The Bedouin asked further;

> "O Allah's Messenger! What is this peak of knowledge?" He said: "It is knowing Allah as He deserves to be known". The Bedouin then asked "And how can He be known as He ought to be?" The Messenger of Allah replied: "It is that you know Him as having no model, no peer, no antithesis and that He is one and only. He is the one who is Apparent yet Hidden, the First and the Last, having no peer or a similitude. This is the true knowledge about Him. (Al-Jibouri 1996: 9)

In summary, the report given above shows that God, as conceived in Islam, is Unique, in such a way that He cannot be compared with any other being.

Names of Allah

The unique name ascribed to God in Islam is Allah. It has no singular or plural form; it also has no gender reflection. It cannot be used for any other being except the Supreme Being. It has a direct emotional and spiritual efficacy which no other word for God can replace especially for Muslims (Abd Allah 2004: 7). The name appears in 2740 times in the Glorious Qur'ān. It is used to express the will of God to mankind. When God was to send Prophet Musa on an errand to Firᶜawn, He said:

> Verily, I am Allah, none has the right to be worshipped but I. So worship Me and perform Aṣ-ṣalāt (canonical worship) for My Remembrance. (Qur'ān 20: 14)

On another occasion relating to the personality of Allah also, the Qur'ān says:

a. Say, (O Muhammad) "He is Allah (the) One.
b. Allah the self-Sufficient Master whom all creatures need.
c. He begets not, nor was He begotten.
d. And there is none co-equal or comparable to Him."

(Qur'ān 112: 1-4)

When denying the Christian doctrine of Trinity and divinity of Prophet ᶜĪsā (Jesus Christ), Islam presents God as one who has no equal or resemblance. The Qur'ān 4: 171 says:

> O people of the scripture (Christians), do not exceed the limits in your religion, nor say of Allah aught but the truth. The Messiah ᶜĪsā (Jesus), son of Maryam (Mary) was (no more than) a messenger of Allah and his word which He bestowed on Maryam and a spirit (Rūḥ) created by Him; so believe in Allah and His messenger. Say not three (trinity). Cease (it is) better for you.For Allah is (the only) one Ilāh (God), glorified is He (far exalted is He) above having a son.

When Allah was addressing Prophet Muhammad in one of the verses of the Glorious Qur'ān, He says: "So know (O Muhammad!) That none has the right to be worshipped except Allah (Qur'ān 47:19)

Chapter four | Faleemu T. M. & Abdu-Raheem M. A, in
Ezenweke, Elizabeth Onyedinma (Ed.)
Whose God Is God? Exploring The Concept Of God Within Religions
London & Abuja, Adonis & Abbey Pulishers

In the case of observing *Ṣalāt* which is the second pillar of Islam and the only mode of worship which distinguishes Muslims from non-Muslims, Allah is the name of God that appears mostly right from *Adhān* (call to prayer), *Allāhu Akbar* (Allah is the Greatest) to the recitation of *Sūratu'l-fātihah* (The Opening Chapter i.e. Chapter 1 of the Qur'ān). At the end of each segment of *Ṣalāt*, *Allāhu Akbar* is pronounced: when bowing (*Rukūʿ*), when prostrating (*Sujūd*), when raising the head from the ground and when rising for the following *Rakʿat*. At the recitation of *At–Tashahhud* (the recital in the last sitting posture of *Ṣalāt*), Allah's name is mentioned. At the end, Muslims terminate the prayer with the famous greeting: *As-Salām ʿalaykum wa raḥmatu'l-Lāh* (May the peace and mercy of Allah be upon you). According to Abd-Allah (2004: 3):

> Etymologically, Allah comes from the same root as the Biblical words Elōhîm, ha-Elōhîm and hā-Elōh (all meaning God). Elōhîm derives from elōh (Hebrew for God), Alāhā is an emphatic form of alāh (Aramaic and Syriac for God) while Allah is connected to ilāh (Arabic for god). All these three names are etymologically equivalent. The variations in their pronunciation can be compared to the one found in Latin, Spanish and Italian words for God (Deus, Dios, and Dio) or the English and German God and Gott. Elōhîm, Alāhā and Allah are all cognates-sister words derived from a common proto-semitic root 'LH, conveying the primary sense of "to worship". The fundamental linguistic meaning of the three Abrahamic cognates for God is "the one who is worshipped".

Concept of Allah

God is conceived in Islam as being absolutely One. This is known in theology as *Tawḥīd* (Islamic Monotheism). To be a true believer in Islam, one has to believe, together with his faith in oneness of Allah, in the existence of His Angels, all the revealed books, all the Messengers sent by Allah to mankind from Adam to Muḥammad (S.A.W), the Day of Resurrection and Destiny. All these together are called the Articles of Faith. Allah says in the Qur'ān 2: 285 as follows:

> The Messenger (Muḥammad S.A.W.) believes in what has been sent down to him from his Lord and (so do) the believers. Each one believes in Allah, His Angels, His Books and His Messengers. (They say) "We make no distinction between one another of His Messengers"…

The absolute unity of God is viewed from three aspects (Al-Badr 2009: 4-5). They are:

I. **Tawḥīd ar-Rubūbiyyah (Unity of Lordship of Allah):** It means to believe that there is only one Lord for all the worlds. Allah alone sustains and cares for all creatures in all aspects. Every reasonable person has a natural disposition for this type of Tawḥīd. This is explained in various verses of the Glorious Qur'ān. Allah says:

> Say (O Muḥammad S.A.W) who provides for you from the sky and the earth? Or who owns hearing and sight? And who brings out the living from the dead and brings out the dead from the living? And who disposes the affairs? "They will say "Allah…" (Qurān'10: 31).

In another verse, Allah says:

> Say "Who is (the) Lord of the seven heavens and (the) Lord of the Great Throne? They will say: "Allah…" Say "Whose the earth is and whosoever is therein? If you know" They will say: "It is Allah…" (Q23: 84-87).

As far as Islam is concerned, based on the Qur'ān, the nature of man leaves him in no doubt that God is the One taking care of the world and providing for all that exists in it. No one contests the lordship of the world with Allah. Firᶜawn (Pharaoh) was (according to the Qur'an) the only one who boldly claimed lordship. He commnded his subjects to worship him instead of the Supreme Being. He was eventually drowned. (Qur'ān 79: 23-25).

The morbid ambition of Firᶜawn (Pharaoh) to be taken as Lord was really a transgression againgt the Almighty God. Many people had ruled over the Egyptians before him. His rulership, therefore, had territorial limitation. He was severely punished. Belief in the fact that God is the Lord responsible for creation is almost universal. Chandhry (2003: 12) says:

> We find out that belief in God is a universal phenomenon. History tells us that such a belief was common to all ages. Even among the Aborigines of Australia and the ancient Maya people of Mexico and Central America, there does exist some sort of belief in an Omnipotent and Ultimate Supreme Being whom they regard as the creator of the universe.

II. **Awḥīd Al-Ulūhiyyah (Oneness of Godhead):** This is oneness in being worthy of worship. This is the total submission to Allah in hope, love, request, supplications and other areas of human endeavors. Most importantly, it means to worship Allah alone without associating any partner with Him either privately or publicly. Nobody, no matter how highly placed, powerful or amazing is an equal to Allah. The Glorious Qur'ān 2: 163 says: "And your God is one, there is none who has the right to be worshipped but He." In another related verse, Allah says:

> Allah bears witness that none has the right to be worshipped but He, and the angels and those having knowledge (also give this witness) (He always) maintains His creation in justice. None has the right to be worshipped but He, the All-Mighty, the All-Wise. (Qur'ān 3: 18).

To worship Allah alone is the rationale behind the creation of man. (Qur'ān 51: 56). All Messengers were sent by Allah to direct mankind towards this course. They all preached the worship of One God. "There is absolutely no evidence from religious history that one God evolved out of many, while there is repeated evidence that many gods were created out of one". (Chaudhry 2003: 15) Ignorance and impatience are some of the reasons which make people deviate from the part of worshipping Allah alone. Allah says (when Prophet Yusuf was addressing his inmates in the prison).

> O two companions of the prison! Are many different lords (gods) better or Allah, the one, the Irresistible? You do not worship besides Him but only names which you have named (forged) - you and your fathers – for which Allah has sent down no authority. (Qur'ān 12: 39-40).

In another verse of the Glorious Qur'ān, Allah mentioned the defense of people who believe in Him but do not worship Him:

> Surely the religion (i.e. worship and obedience) is for Allah only. And those who take (protectors, helpers, lords, gods) besides Him (say): "We worship them only that they may bring us near to Allah" (Qur'ān 39: 3)

It is with this aspect of believe (oneness in obedience and worship) that Allah categorizes people into believers and non-believers. Worshipping any other except Allah or with Him is polytheism; the highest rank of disobedience in Islam and the only unforgivable sin in the sight of Allah (if one dies without repentance). Allah says in the Qur'ān:

> Verily, Allah forgives not that partners should be set up with Him (in worship), but He forgives except that (anything else) to whom He wills; and whosoever sets up partners with Allah (in worship), he has indeed invented a tremendous sin. (Qur'ān 4:48).

When Junayd (a Ṣūfi (mystic) leader and scholar) was asked the meaning of Tawḥīd (Monotheism) he said: "It is total belief in oneness of Allah who begets not nor is He begotten, with no partner, no associate, no adaptation nor any representation". (Al-Qushri: 2005: 280). Also, Shaykh Abdul-Qadri Jaylani said: "Allah is one and He loves that which is united and one. He wants all worship and all righteous acts, which He considers as devotion, to belong to Himself alone. (Al-Jilani n.d.: 20)

III. **Tawḥīd al-Asmā' wa'ṣ-Ṣifāt (Unity in Names and Attributes).** The attributes of Allah are the names of Allah formed from His actions and divine qualities. They are uncountable because it is Allah who is behind every action or occurrence; hence, from every action, the actor has a name. His many names have great efficacy and constitute a special channel of spirituality. Allah says in the Qur'ān: "To Allah belong all the Most Beautiful Names; so call on Him by name (Qur'ān 7: 180). Collectively, these names affirm the supreme perfection of Allah and inspire deeper understanding of His beauty and majesty (Abd-Allah 2004: 4). All the attributes of Allah are perfect and unique. It is part of Islamic belief that none of these attributes can be used for any other being in its perfect form except Allah because nothing resembles Him. (Qur'ān 42: 11).

Attributes of Allah: Among the names are the following:

Ar-Rahmān: (the Most Gracious): It appears 57 times in the Qur'ān. It is from the root form *"Rahmah"* (Grace). It symbolizes the unlimited grace of Allah which He bestows on the universe and all creatures so much that they continue to live peacefully and harmoniously without unnecessary challenges (Chaudhry 2003: 5). Prayers for special grace are addressed to Allah by invoking this important name of His. The Qur'ān says:

> (O Muhammad) invoke Allah or invoke *Ar-Raḥmān* (the Most Gracious), by whatever name you invoke Him (it is the same) for to Him belong the Best Names… (Qur'ān 17: 110)

This attribute is invoked to show the great works of Allah. Chapter 55 of the Qur'ān is named *Ar-Raḥmān*. In this Chapter, the special grace of Allah to man is elucidated. Among other things, the revelation of the Qur'ān is mentioned. It is the criterion to differentiate between truth and falsehood. It guides those who believe in it to the straight path leading to self-fulfilment in this world and admission into *Al-Jannah* in the hereafter. Another special grace mentioned is the gift of language and ability to express oneself intelligibly and eloquently. This endowment is one of the basic features that distinguish human beings from other animals. In fact, the Arabs refer to man as *ḥayawān nāṭiq* (animal with the ability to talk). This is apparently with reference to the fact that without the ability to speak, man can hardly be distinguished from other animals.

Ar-Raḥīm: **(The Most Merciful):** This is another prominent name of Allah. It appears along with *Ar-Raḥmān* in the opening of all chapters of the Glorious Qur'ān (except Chapter 9). Both names are derived from Arabic word 'Raḥmah' which is closely related to *Rahim*, the word for womb and fecundity (Abdul-Hakim n.d. 5). Besides its usual appearance at the beginning of all chapters the name, '*Ar-Raḥīm*,' appears in 125 places in the Qur'ān. It symbolizes salvation, mercy and compassion of Allah. In most verses of the Qur'ān where it appears, it also goes with another name of Allah '*Al-Ghafūr*' (the Forgiver of sins).

Al-Malik: **(the Supreme Owner, the King):** This is one of the names of Allah mentioned in the Qur'ān. It appears as *Malik* (without the definite article) in the Qur'ān 1: 4 and 3: 26 and as *Al-Malik* (the King) in Qur'ān 59: 23, 62: 1 and 114: 2. That Allah is the Supreme Owner implies that He is independent of anything that exists while everything depends on Him. He is the Sole Owner of the world and the King in His Majesty presiding over all the affairs of the world. He is going to preside over the final judgment on the Last Day (Qur'ān 1: 4).

Al-Quddūs: (The Holy) This is another attribute of Allah mentioned in the Qur'ān. Allah describes Himself with it in two places in the Qur'ān, that is, Qur'ān 59: 23 and Qur'ān 62: 1. His holiness is such that distances Him from all unworthy qualities disbelievers wrongly ascribe to Him.

As-Salām: (The One Free from all defects), *Al-Mu'min* (The Giver of security) and *Al-Muhaymin* (The Watcher over His creatures), are some of the beautiful names of Allah which appear in the Qur'ān. They are mentioned along with other names to describe Allah. The Qur'ān says:

> He is Allah beside whom none has the right to be worshipped but He, the Holy, the One free from all defects, the Giver of security, the Watcher over His creatures... (Qur'ān 59: 29).

Al-ᶜAzīz: (The All-Mighty) is another beautiful name of Allah. Allah describes His mightiness in 95 different verses of Holy Qur'ān. He is so Power that nobody can query His authority. What He wants, He does. No power can force Him to do what He does not want to do.

Al-Jabbār: (the Compeller) and *Al- Mutakabbir*: (the Supreme): These are two of Allah's attributes which appear in the Qur'ān. Both names appear once in the Qur'ān as Allah's attributes. They imply that nothing can resist His power which governs and regulates all existence. (Abdul-Hakim n.d. 5) (Qur'ān 59: 23).

Al-Khāliq:- (the Creator), *Al-Bāri'* (the Inventor) and *Al-Musawwir* (the Fashioner) are other three names of Allah used together in the Qur'ān. Allah created everything that exists and He absolves Himself from any blemish. There is perfect harmony in what He has created. There is absolutely no incongruity or discord in His creation. He is the Originator of all things. He designs everything the way He wants it to look like without copying the idea from elsewhere. Things that are big are big because Allah wants them to be big and things that are small are made so by Him. He shapes creatures in accordance with the nature He wishes them to have. Everything in the world has its purpose and is moulded to serve that purpose. Some creatures are made in the form of liquid such as water and blood; some are created in the solid form like hills and mountains. He created animals in different species and fashions them in ways that suit His majesty. All animals, including man, who live on land and in the sea and birds that soar in the skies are created in the best form and Allah has bestowed upon them such qualities that are best suited to their particular purposes and needs (Chaudhry 2003: 11). The Glorious Qur'ān 24: 45 says:

> Allah has created every moving (living) creature from water. Of them there are some that creep on their bellies, and some that walk on legs and some that walk on four. Allah creates what He wills. Allah is able to do all things.

Al-Laṭīf: (The Most Subtle) and *Al-Khabīr* (The Well-Acquainted) are another two attributes of Allah mentioned in the Qur'ān. Both names appear six times in the Qur'ān. They refer to Allah's magnanimity over His creatures. Allah showers abundant care and kindness on all the creatures. He knows their needs and aspirations even before they request for them. He is also Well-Acquainted with their deeds, whether in secret or in the open.

Al-Ḥafīẓ: (the Protector) and *Al-ᶜAlīm* (the All- Knower) are other two divine attributes of Allah mentioned in the Qur'ān. The first attribute shows that Allah takes good care of His creatures and safeguards them against dangers. Most of such dangers are not known to the creatures not to talk of the possibility of taking preventive measures to avoid them. The second shows the all-encompassing knowledge of Allah. The past, the present and the future are known to Him with certainty. He does not forget or fail to take note of anything happening at any point in time or anywhere.

Al-Ḥaqq: (the Truth): This is another beautiful name of Allah. Allah is the Truth and man has been given a mind capable of understanding the Truth, a will capable of choosing the path of the Truth and a heart inclined by its very nature to love the Truth. To deny Allah is to distance oneself from the Truth. Any person who falls into this error has chosen to ignore the Truth. He has prevented himself from seeing what is ultimately self-evident (Chaudhry 2003: 20).

Allah says in the Qur'ān:

> Have We not made for him (man) two eyes, And a tongue and two lips, And shown him the two ways (good and evil). (Qur'ān 90: 8-9)

An-Nūr: (the Light) is another attribute of Allah. He is the Light of the world physically, spiritually and intellectually. Physically, Allah regulates the inter-change of day and night. He makes light appear during the day and brings about darkness during the night. The Qur'ān 17: 12 asserts:

> And We have appointed the night and the day as two signs. Then We have obliterated the sign of the night (with darkness) while We have made the sign of the day illuminating, that you may seek bounty from your Lord,… (Qur'ān 17: 12).

The spiritual light of Allah is Islamic Monotheism. (Qur'ān 9: 32). Whoever is rightly guided to the path should be thankful to Allah. Intellectually, Allah endowed man with a sense of reasoning and shed His light on it. It is left for man to use it positively or negatively. Whoever is deprived of any aspect of light by Allah cannot get it elsewhere. Allah says in the Qur'ān:

> Allah is the Light of the heavens and the earth…. (Qur'ān 24: 35)
> …And for he whom Allah has not appointed light, there is no light. (Qur'ān 24: 40)

Al-ᶜAfuww: (the Pardoner of Sins), ***At-Tawwāb*** (The Accepter of Repentance) and ***Al-Ghaffār*** (the Ever Forgiving) are other attributes of Allah in the Glorious Qur'ān. The three attributes emphasise the kindness of Allah to pardon, forgive and accept repentance. They give hope to sinners for Allah's mercy. No matter the gravity of offence committed by any individual or a group during their lifetime, they can turn to Allah for forgiveness. He accepts sincere repentance but not after death. The Glorious Qur'ān 4: 48 says:

> And of no effect is the repentance of those who continue to do evil deeds until death faces one of them and he says: 'Now I repent,' nor those who die while they are disbelievers.

Al-Hādī: (the Guide): This is another beautiful attribute of Allah. He sent Messengers to each hamlet, tribe or nation to direct people to obey Him and follow the path that leads to eternal pleasure. He revealed scriptures to show the right and wrong paths. All these are in addition to the senses every human being has which go a long way to enable him to distinguish righteous deeds from evils.

As-Samīᶜ (the Hearer) and *Al-Baṣīr* (The Seer) are two of Allah's attributes in the Glorious Qur'ān. Allah hears every sound including the footsteps of ants and things that are in the grave. Likewise, His vision has no limit. The tongue, eyes and ears are instruments created by Allah to suit the limited capabilities of His creatures while His unlimited capabilities do not need such. (Chaudhry 2003: 19)

Al-Awwal (The First) and *Al-Ākhir* (The Last) are also attributes of Allah in the Glorious Qur'ān. He has no beginning because He began all things and He has no end because it is He who shall put an end to everything. The time He started creation is only known to Him and when and how everything shall end is in His knowledge.

Aẓ-Ẓāhir (The Apparent), *Al-Bāṭin* (the Hidden), *Al-Aḥad* (The Only One) and *Al-ᶜAliyy* (The Most High) are among the beautiful names of Allah. He is Apparent in the sense that His works in creation prove His existence even though no eye can see Him. He is Hidden because He is beyond the reach of sense of sight, hearing or feeling. He is the Only One, Indivisible. He is Higher than anything which people equate Him with. (Abdu-Hakim n.d. 25)

Although some of these names are occasionally used to describe certain personalities in the Qur'ān, such usage cannot in any form be matched with Allah's name. Examples are Prophet Muhammad qualified as (*Raḥīm*) (Merciful) (Qur'ān 9: 128), Yusuf calling himself Protector with full knowledge (*Ḥafīẓ*, *ᶜAlīm*) (Qur'ān 12: 55) and his brothers calling him *Al-ᶜAzīz* (Qur'ān 12: 78 & 88). The interpretations of these names whenever they are used for any other being except Allah are at the level of imperfection of man. Nobody has the qualities as possessed by Him in their perfect form.

Nature of Allah

To describe the nature of Allah in Islam is beyond what anyone can comprehend. He can only be described the way He has described Himself or has been described by His Messenger. Allah says in the Qur'ān:

> Allah! None has the right to be worshipped but He, the Ever living, the one Who sustains and protects all that exists. Neither slumber nor sleep overtakes Him. To Him belongs whatever is in the heavens and whatever is on the earth. Who is he that can intercede with Him except with His permission? He knows what happens to them (His creatures) in this world and what will happen to them in the Hereafter. And they will never compass anything of His knowledge except that which He wills. His *kursiy* (chair, authority) extends over the heavens and the earth and He feels no fatigue in guarding and preserving them. And He is the Most High, the Most Great. (Qur'ān 2: 255)

As enunciated in this verse, Allah is Ever-Living. This indicates that He is a living God Who will never die. He created life and death (Qur'ān 67: 2). He takes life from whoever He wishes and gives life to whoever He wishes (Qur, ān 3: 156, 7: 158, 9: 116, 10: 56, 53: 44). He can never die because He created death and when all things perish including death itself, Allah shall be the only One remaining. (Qur'ān 28: 88, 55: 26-27). When everything has been caused by Allah to come to an end, He will then ask:

> Whose is the kingdom this Day? (Allah Himself will reply to His question). It is Allah's the One, the Irresistible (Qur'ān 40: 16).

That Allah is the Protector and Sustainer of all things that exist is another testimony to His unlimited power. He never and shall never doss not talk of sleeping. Allah created sleep for some of His

---

Chapter four | Faleemu T. M. & Abdu-Raheem M. A, in
Ezenweke, Elizabeth Onyedinma (Ed.)
Whose God Is God? Exploring The Concept Of God Within Religions
London & Abuja, Adonis & Abbey Pulishers

creatures to regain strength after stress so that tiredness or fatigue cannot overtake Allah. When a man sleeps, he loses the greater part of his senses. Everything he is doing comes to a standstill until he wakes up. Every second of life is a busy period for Allah. If He could sleep like man does, the entire universe will collapse. Allah says:

> Whosoever is in the heavens and on earth begs of Him (his needs from Him). Everyday He is (engaged) in some affairs (such as giving honour or disgrace to some, life or death to some, etc.) (Qur'ān 55: 29).

To Allah belongs whatever is in the heavens and whatever is on earth and beneath it. Allah owns everything in creation. He created everything that exists, whether visible or invisible. Allah created human beings and endows are physically, materially, spiritually and intellectually. With such endowments, He can think and manufacture things. Allah says:

> Verily, We have created man from *Nutfah* (drop) of mixed semen (sexual discharge of man and woman), in order to try him; so we made him to hear and see. Verily, we showed him the way, whether he be grateful or ungrateful. (Qur'ān 76: 2-3).

To Allah belongs the exclusive power and authority over the universe. He does not need consultation before He takes any action and cannot be rebuked or reprimanded by anybody for any decision He takes. Everything that exists – everything that happens – is subject to His control; there is nothing that competes with Him or that escapes His grasp. (Abdul-Hakim n.d. 2). (See also Qur'ān 5: 18, 5: 120, 9: 116, 24: 42, 42: 49, 43: 85, 48: 14, 68: 1 and 85: 9).

The power to grant the opportunity to intercede on behalf of other people on the Day of Judgment belongs to Allah. The Qur'ān 21: 28 declares: "He knows what is before them and what is behind them, and they cannot intercede except for him with whom He is pleased. And they stand in awe for fear of Him". Allah is Omniscient. He knows what happens to every creature before it happens as well as what shall be the aftermath (Qur'ān 6: 59). Nothing transcends the knowledge of Allah, He knows everything. "And (whether) you keep your talk secret or disclose it, verily He is All-knower of what is in the breasts (of man). (Qur'ān 67: 13)

Only what Allah wants to be made known to his creatures at every point in time is known to them. The knowledge of Allah is broad and beyond human comprehension. Allah Himself says that He has bestowed on human beings only a small part of knowledge (Qur'ān 17: 85). Allah also says:

> Say (O Muhammad to mankind) "If the sea were ink for (writing) the words of my Lord, surely, the sea would be exhausted before the word of My Lord would be finished, even if We brought (another sea) like it for its aid. (Qur'ān18:109).

Another verse says:

> And if all the trees on the earth were pen and the sea (were ink wherewith to write) with seven seas behind it to add to its (supply) yet the words of Allah would not be exhausted. Verily Allah is All-Mighty, All-Wise. (Qur'ān 31: 27)

From the vast knowledge of Allah, He gave Prophet Adam the knowledge of names with which he gained supremacy over Angels and Allah made them bow for him (Qur'ān 2: 31-34).

Since Allah has been existing before anything (including the Throne) whoever thinks that Allah is on something or from something or in something has associated partners with Allah because if He is on something, it implies that He is supported. Likewise if He is from something, it implies that He is created and if He is in something, it means that He is confined (As-Safuri n.d. 7). Ali bn Abi Talib (may Allah be pleased with him) was asked; "Where is our Lord or is there a specific place for Him?" Ali replied: "Your question 'Where is God' is asking about space. God has been existing when there was no space. He later created time and space."(Al-Hasani 2008: 71)

The *Kursiy* (chair) of Allah extends over the heavens and the earth. Prophet Muhammad was reported to have said: "The *Kursiy* compared to the ʿ*Arsh* is nothing but like a ring thrown out upon space of the desert" (Al-Hilali and Khan 2004: 57). Guiding and preserving the heaven and the earth is no burden to Allah. What else

---

Chapter four | Faleemu T. M. & Abdu-Raheem M. A, in
Ezenweke, Elizabeth Onyedinma (Ed.)
Whose God Is God? Exploring The Concept Of God Within Religions
London & Abuja, Adonis & Abbey Pulishers

then could burden Him? Nothing, because He is the Most High, the Most Great.

Among the nature of Allah is that He cannot be seen here on earth. "No vision can grasp Him, but He grasps all visions. He is the Most Subtle and Courteous, the Well-Acquainted (with all things)" (Qur'ān 6: 103). When Prophet Mūsā sought permission from Allah to see Him, Allah replied:

> "You cannot see Me but look upon the mountain. If it stands in its place, then you shall see Me". So when his Lord appeared to the mountain, He made it melt to dust and Musa fell down unconscious. When he recovered his senses, he said: Glorified are you, I turn to you in repentance and I am the first of the believers. (Qur'ān 7: 143).

Myths of Origin

Islam teaches that Allah has no historical source. He is the only one who knows when He has been existing. He has no beginning and has no end. A philosophical expression in this respect states that "Allah is the First Cause, the only Cause and the Uncaused Cause (Abdul-Hakim n.d. 2). This agrees with the Qur'ān 57: 3 which says:

> He is the First (nothing is before Him) and the Last (nothing comes after Him) and Most High (nothing is above Him) and Most Near (nothing is nearer than He). And He is All-Knower of everything.

In a Ḥadīth narrated by ʿImrān bin Ḥusain, the Prophet (S. A. W.) is reported to have said: "There was nothing but Allah and His throne was over the water and He wrote everything in the book (in the heaven) and created the heavens and the earth."(Khan 1996: 640). How and when Allah created Himself goes beyond human reasoning and understanding. What is clearly known is that everything that exists has been created by Allah. On the creation of heavens and earth, the Qur'ān 57: 4 says: "He it is who created the heavens and the earth in six days...

In another verse, Allah says:

> Then He completed and finished their creation (as) seven heavens in two days and He made in each heaven its affairs. And We adorned the nearest (lowest) heaven with lamp (stars) to be an adornment as well as to guard (from the devils by using them as missiles against them). Such is the decree of the All-Mighty, the All-Knower. (Qur'ān 41: 12)

On the creation of man and jinn, Allah says: "He created man (Adam) from sounding clay like the clay of pottery. And the Jinn; He created from a smokeless flame of fire" (Qur'ān 55: 14-15).

Allah explains the developmental processes which the creation of human beings takes in the Holy Quran. (Qur'ān 23: 12-14). The period which these developmental processes take in each stage in the mother's womb till it becomes a new born baby was narrated in a tradition of Prophet Muhammad:

> The creation of each of you was gathered in his mother's womb for forty days as *Nuṭfah* (mixed drops of the male and female sexual discharge), then it turns into a clot (a piece of thick coagulated blood) for the same length of time (forty days), then it turns into a little lump of flesh for the same length of time, and an angel is sent to him. *Rūḥ* (soul or breath of life) is breathed into it... (Muslim 1995: 2643)

Modern scientific proofs have attested to what Allah and His Messenger said about two centuries ago. The power of Allah to create has not been contested by anyone. Several verses of the Glorious Qur'ān attest to the fact that every creation originates from Allah. He is not only the Creator, He is the Originator who created the heavens and earth and everything therein from His glory. (Qur'ān 6: 14, 6: 79, 12: 101, 14: 10, 21: 56, 35: 10 and 35: 46).

Subordinate

Allah has no associate to consult or receive assistance from. To affiliate such to Him is a grievous sin in the sight of Allah and a threat to Islamic Monotheism. Allah says in the Glorious Qur'ān 31: 13 that:

> "...Verily, joining others in worship with Allah is a great wrong indeed.

Conclusion

The Arabic word for God is Allah. Therefore, Muslims refer to Him as such. The most distinctive feature of the concept of God in Islam is belief in the absolute and indivisible unity of Allah. He is One in His Essence, Works and Attributes. The concept is encapsulated in *Kalimatu'sh-Shahādah* (Word of Testimony) the utterance of which qualifies one to be admitted into Islam. It states that there is no deity or being worthy of worship beside Allah and that Muḥammad is His Messenger. The statement rules out completely the possibility of having any other object of worship beside, instead or along with Allah. Such practices amount to *Shirk* (associating partner[s] with Allah), the direct opposite of *Tawḥīd* (belief in the unity of Allah) which forms the bedrock of the teachings and practices in Islam.

Judging from the concept, nature, historical origin and all the attributes of Allah, it is obvious that He is the only God who deserves to be worshipped. He also recommended the mode He should be worshipped which anything outside it shall not be regarded as an act of worship.

References

Abd-Allah, Umar Faruq (2004). *One God Many Names*, n.p. Nawawi Foundation.

Abdul-Hakīm, Hassan (Gai Eaton), (n.d.) *The Concept of God in Islam*. www.holybook.com/wp.../The-concept-of-Allah-in-Islam.pdg p.9 Retrieved on 15.3.2013

Al-Badr, Abdu-Razaq Abdul-Muhsin (2009). *Al-Mukhtasar al-Mufīd fi bayān Dalā'il Aqsām at-Tawḥīd* Madina: King Fahd Publishing co.

Al-Hasani, Ibn ᶜAjibah (2008). *Iqāz Al-Himam Fi Sharih Al-Hikam*. Lebanon: Dār-Al-kotob Al-Ilmiyya.

Al-Hilali, Muhammad Taqi-ud-Din and Khan, Muhammad Muhsin (2004). Madinah, King Fahd Complex for the Printing of the Holy Qur'an

Al-Jibouri, Yasin (1996). *The Concept of God in Islam (A Selection)*, U.S.A.: Ansariyan Publications.

Al-Jilāni, Shaykh Abdul-Qadri (n.d.) *The Secrets of Secrets and The Manifestation of Lights*, n.p., n.p.

Al-Qushri, Abu Qāsim Abdul-Karīm bn Hawāsin (2005). *Risālat Al-Qushri fi ᶜIlmi At-Tasawwuf*. Lebanon: Dārul-kitab.

As-Safuri, Abdu-Rahmān (n.d.) *Nazhatul-Majālis wa Muntakhabu Nafā'is*, n.p., Darul-Fiqr.

Chaudhry, Rashid Ahmad (2003). *My Book About God*, Islamabad, Islam International Publication.

Khan, Muhammad Muhsin (Translator) (1996) *Sahīh Al-Bukhāri Summarized*.

Riyādh: Dār-us-Salām.Muslim, Imam (1995) *Sahih Muslim* Beirut: Dar al-Kutub al-ᶜIlmiyyah

CHAPTER FIVE

God and the New Age Movement

Luis Santamaría del Río

Introduction

When approaching the New Age (NA) movement in the beliefs panorama of the current world, Joseph Ratzinger went further than the mere analysis of the phenomenon when he considered that the matter of God is the key to knowing and understanding the doctrines and practices, and also to be able to evaluate its diffusion. Apart from its Gnostic character, the German theologian, Cardinal at that time, emphasized the NA mystic: "The Absolute is not to be believed, but to be experienced. God is not a person to be distinguished from the world, but a spiritual energy present in the universe. Religion in the words of Ratzinger (2004), means "the harmony of oneself with the cosmic whole; the overcoming of all separations" (pp. 126-131). This is a good summary of the concept of God held by new religiosity, and it reflects its energetic, individualist and impersonal character. However, it is necessary to go deeper into the different modalities that can be found in such a diffuse and complex reality as the NA. In order to do this, the focus of this paper will center on certain authors and trends considered important so as to be able to obtain a sample sufficient representation of the doctrines of this new religiosity.

Alice A. Bailey: The Deity of all Human Beings

One of the main sources of the theological doctrine of the NA can be found in the field of contemporaneous esotericism. Bailey (1964) explicitly announced the second coming of Christ as the World Instructor in the New Age by the end of the 20th century. In her work, *Problems of Humanity*, She (Bailey, 1964) states that: "We can recognize the timelessness of faith and the witness of the Spirit, down the countless ages to the *fact of God*" (p. 122). She later explains: "The fact of God, the fact of Christ, the fact of men's spiritual approach to divinity, the fact of the deathlessness of the Spirit, the fact of spiritual opportunity and the fact of man's relation to God and to his fellowmen –upon these we can take our stand" (p. 122).

What does Bailey mean when she talks about God? Regarding his identity, she maintains that the new world religion, that which is to be brought about by the NA, must create a synthesis of the immanent God of the eastern religions and the transcendent God of the western ones. That is, "God, greater than the created whole, yet God present also in the part; God transcendent guarantees the plan for our world and is the purpose, conditioning all lives from the minutest atom, up through all the kingdoms of nature to man" (p. 142). The author reiterates the idea of the immanence of God in the universe in that book and, although she refers to an external reality to the man, she includes it, after all, in the human being.

God makes he present in man's heart and, for this reason , all historic revelation written down loses its value. The Bailey doctrine ends with the claim of the great religion having been received as a direct revelation from God. Bailey (1964) asserts that:

> The doctrine of the verbal inspiration of the Scriptures of the world (deemed particularly applicable to the Christian Bible) is today completely exploded and with it the infallibility of interpretation; ... dogmas and doctrines, theology and dogmatic affirmations, do not necessarily indicate the truth as it exists in the mind of God, with Whose mind the majority of dogmatic interpreters claim familiarity. Theology is simply what men *think* is in the mind of God. (p. 129).

God is incomprehensible on one hand but on the other hand, the truth can be known, the truth being that which is common to all religions and, hence, she says that the key to truth lies in the unifying power of Comparative Religion. (Bailey, 1964).

At the bottom of it there is a perception of the deeply individualist and far from institutionalized spirituality. An objective revelation has not been given to any certain human community, and God is revealed in man's heart. By reading Bailey's work, we discover the true human knowledge of the Deity: "The revelation of the nature of God has been a slow unfolding process, paralleled by the evolutionary growth of the human consciousness" (pp. 140-141). Even more, God not only reveals himself in men, but also the men themselves identify with the Supreme Being, as Bailey asserts on several occasions. Bailey (1964) asserts that: "The spirit in man is undying; it forever endures, progressing from point to point and stage to stage upon the path of evolution, unfolding steadily and sequentially the divine attributes and aspects" (p. 142). Continuing, Bailey (1964) added that: "The fact of this innate divinity explains the urge at the heart of every man for betterment, for experience, for progress, for increasing realization and for his steady moving on towards the distant height which he has vision…. Therefore, eventually the new world religion "will produce a humanity which will recognize the divine in all men, at varying stages of expression" (pp. 143-145).

Furthermore, 'Divine Approaches' is discussed as special moments in history where God approaches humanity. However, they are not just the consequence of a simple dynamic of God's grace, but they also come from a great human effort. There have been several periods whereby the coming of the Christ of the NA, is anticipated. Each of these Approaches means an advance in the knowledge of the reality of the Supreme Being. In the end, this 'expansive wave' of the Deity exceeds the human, reaching a pantheist situation, which can be observed when this esoteric author states that in this double game of the transcendence-immanence, God is immanent in all the things created and there is an innate divinity in everything that exists, presided by the human being and its "inherent divinity. (Bailey, 1964).

Lastly, it is worthy to emphasize the relationship of the human being with the Deity. This can be summarized in the invocation and the spiritual practices that combine all the worship, praying and meditation activities of religions that will enable mankind to function under the control of the inner divinity, or interior spiritual man; this training will also reveal to them the fact of God immanent in all forms. Thus, having passed from the cultural way of addressing to the Supreme Being as something external to a practice that acknowledges the immanence of the Deity in the human being, the potency of worship as an act of invocative approach to God will prove amazing and miraculous in its results.

However, in response to whether or not the Ascended Masters, whose existence, in the Theosophy understanding of the world, she widely promoted in her work are divine beings. Bailey, who wrote most of her work inspired by one of these Ascended Masters, Djwhal Khul, answered that they are not gods. Sutcliffe (2007) quoting Alice Bailey's book titled Ascended Masters explains that ascended masters are "God-realized beings, whether embodied or disembodied, beings who have progressed a bit further than some of us and models for the advanced human being" (pp. 68-69).

In a nutshell, Bailey (1964) makes a good synthesis of the contributions of the esoteric field to NA spirituality. The Theosophy legacy can be found in her works, but she also incorporates other important spiritual trends for the present paper, which will be explained in detail in the coming sections, specifically; Christian Science and New Thought.

From Christian Science to the New Thought

In a brief summary of all of these spiritual trends that nourish the NA, the starting point will be, due to its importance, Christian Science, founded by Mary Baker Eddy (1821-1910). Her protestant religious experience was influenced by the healing attributed to reading the Bible, which caused the creation of a different religious group, which gives her book *Science and Health with Key to the Scriptures* the value to interpret biblical teachings. In this book, the references to the Deity are personal, but with a wide definition of the biblical concept of God. Thus, one can read in the book's glossary the following summary of the meaning of the term God: "The great I AM; the all-knowing, all-seeing, all-acting, all-wise, all-loving, and eternal; Principle; Mind; Soul; Spirit; Life; Truth; Love; all substance; intelligence" (Eddy, 1910). Although Christian Science, as it has already been said, was born into reformed Christianity, it rejects the Trinitarian doctrine of God. Eddy (1910) states that "the theory of three persons in one God (that is, a personal Trinity or Tri-unity) suggests polytheism, rather than the

Chapter five	Luis Santamaría del Río, in
	Ezenweke, Elizabeth Onyedinma (Ed.)
	Whose God Is God? Exploring The Concept Of God Within Religions
	London & Abuja, Adonis & Abbey Pulishers

one ever-present I AM" (p. 256). She refers to God as Father-Mother, and she insists on moving Him away from matter. God is spiritual and man, made in His own image, is, above all, spirit, soul, mind, thought...without any corporal or material value. Therefore, theology completely determines the anthropology of this spiritual trend as well as its comprehension of reality, since, as a last resort, Christian Science states that evil and illnesses do not exist; they are a product of the mind. The doctrinal argument supporting this statement is simple: God is spirit, truth, and love, and God is real; therefore, everything that is not spirit, truth, or love does not have any entity, because it is not of God; it is not real.

She considers Christ as Son of God and Messiah, as well as a model to inspire all believers, but stripped of divinity. Man can advance in a deification process, like Jesus did: "God expresses in man the infinite idea forever developing itself, broadening and rising higher and higher from a boundless basis. Mind manifests all that exists in the infinitude of Truth. We know no more of man as the true divine image and likeness, than we know of God" (Eddy, 1910). However, there is no fusion of man with God, since man keeps his personality.

A movement close to Christian Science is the conglomerate named New Thought (see Mosley, 2006), within the metaphysical trend of esotericism, also halfway between the nineteenth and twentieth centuries, which "has finally culminated into the New Age, something logical given its conception and ideas" (Guerra, 1998). They advocate the idea of God as a higher reason or transcendental intuition that leads to Pantheism; a nature in which was immanent the One Spirit of the Universe; a universe animated by a Universal Mind, proceeding under Universal Law and Order" (Atkinson, 2009). This movement goes a step further regarding Christian Science, and talks about an impersonal Deity, a universal mind that impregnates everything, energy, or, to sum up, the power we call God. (Hunting, 1934).

With similar words to those already seen in Christian Science, one can read in one systematic book of the New Thought that it teaches the existence of a Supreme Power back of, underlying and in all things. This Supreme Power is Infinite, Illimitable, Eternal and Unchangeable. It is, has always been, and always will be. It is Omnipresent (present everywhere); Omnipotent (all powerful, possessing all the power that is); and Omniscient (all-knowing, all-seeing, knowing everything, seeing everything (Atkinson, 2010). As a consequence, everything is part of a large unity (therefore, one of the main movements of the New Thought is the so-called Unity School of Christianity), and the whole Universe is an emanation from God.

One can get to know God, according to the New Thought representatives. However, on this point, one can see again that due to their philosophical background of modernity, religion and science are mixed up. This is evident in the merging of their Pantheist conception of reality, deity and nature. For some adherents of the NA, the laws of the universe are the laws of God. Science, then, in its broadest aspect is a search for the knowledge of God. (Allen, 1914). Furthermore, the human being is immortal. All religions have a vocation for a future unification as corroborated by NA and in the end, for a final disappearance, due to the unity of all the reality and to the uniqueness of God. Trine (1910) opines that:

> The view of God in regard to which we are agreed, that He is the Infinite Spirit of Life and Power that is back of all, which is working in and through all, that is the life of all, is a matter in regard to which all men, all religions can agree. With this view there can be no infidels or atheists. (p. 204).

As in Christian Science, Jesus of Nazareth is a chosen one, in whom the spiritual figure of the Christ is personified, but he is not the Deity made flesh as Christianity asserts. In this way, the founder of the Unity School of Christianity, Fillmore (1946) explains that Jesus understood that "the Christ, the divine-idea man or Word of God, was His true self and that He was consequently the Son of God. Because Jesus held to this perfect image of the divine man, the Christ or Word entered consciously into every atom of His being, even to the very cells of His outer organism, and transformed all His body into pure, immortal, spiritual substance and life" (p. 15).

Chapter five | Luis Santamaría del Río, in
Ezenweke, Elizabeth Onyedinma (Ed.)
Whose God Is God? Exploring The Concept Of God Within Religions
London & Abuja, Adonis & Abbey Pulishers

This strict monotheism of an impersonal God needs to apply an allegorical and symbolical interpretation to the Christian doctrine of the Trinity. Holmes (1926) explains the threefold nature of God that:

> God is Spirit, or Self-Knowingness; God is Law and action; and God is Result or Body. This is the inner meaning of the teaching of 'the Trinity'. ... A trinity of being appears to run through all nature and all Life (p. 43).

The God of Spiritualism

The National Spiritualist of Churches lacks a homogeneous doctrine and this can also be applied to their dogmatic content about God. However, the great majority of spiritualist movements agree to acknowledge the existence of an Infinite Intelligence, as can be seen in one of their foundational documents. Lewis (2004) states that:

> The Declaration of principles, published in 1899 in Chicago by the National Spiritualist Association of Churches (NSAC): "1. we believe in Infinite Intelligence. 2. We believe that the phenomena of Nature, both physical and spiritual, are the expression of Infinite Intelligence. 3. We affirm that a correct understanding of such expression and living in accordance therewith constitute true religion" (pp. 510-511).

The third president of the NSAC, Joseph P. Whitwell, comments on the two first principles; first, by this we express our belief in a supreme Impersonal Power, everywhere present, manifesting as life, through all forms of organized matter, called by some, God, by others, Spirit and by Spiritualists, Infinite Intelligence and secondly, in this manner we express our belief in the immanence of Spirit and that all forms of life are manifestations of Spirit or Infinite Intelligence, and thus that all men are children of God. It is, therefore, clear that there is a common doctrinal foundation for all Spiritualism followers, even for the denomination of Deity. (NSAC website).

Similarly, spiritualist authors still use a Trinitarian Christian language about God, but they empty it from its original meaning, and apply it to their anthropology. One such instance can be observed in the statements of Peebles (2003) that:

Spiritualists, like the primitive Christians, believe in God the Father and in the brotherhood of the races. They acknowledge the living Christ; they feel the influx of the Holy Spirit... Evidently man is a Trinity in unity, constituted of a physical body, a soul, or soul body, and a conscious, undying spirit–one uncompounded, indestructive divine substance– the Divine Ego ... God is love, for spiritualists, and He is spirit, which determines the spiritual composition of every reality; the corner Stone, the foundation pillar of Spiritualism is Spirit, and God is Spirit, essential and immutable" (pp. 8 - 11).

If we look at one of the main representatives of contemporaneous Spiritualism, its medium, Allan Kardec, father of the French branch of this movement, starts his *The Spirits' Book*, reflecting on the nature and existence of God, just like the traditional catechism (with questions and answers). He talks about God as Supreme Intelligence, following the tradition of Spiritualism, and he states that the first cause of everything existing is an Intelligent Power. Regarding man's chances to truly know God, Kardec (2006) writes that "the inferiority of the human faculties renders it impossible for man to comprehend the essential nature of God" (p. 65). He goes on to say that God is eternal, unchangeable, immaterial, unique, all-powerful, and sovereignly just and good. The author rejects Pantheism, since God is cause, and he cannot be confused with the effects or mixed up with the matter.

Contradicting the Christian classic rejection of spiritualist practices, firmly based on the biblical tradition, Kardec (2010), like other authors within this movement, states that if spirits communicate with men it is because God sends them or, at least, allows them to get in contact with one another. In a conversation with a priest, Kardec (2010) states that "all religions say the same thing; Protestantism, Judaism, Islam, as well as Catholicism... The Spirits proclaim a sole God who is supremely just and good" (p. 128). In short, Spiritualism considers itself the new religion that overcomes and unifies all of them and, therefore, has the true doctrine of God. Following this line of reasoning, when Kardec (2010) explains the practices of invoking the spirits as "We call them in God's name because we believe in God and we know that nothing is done in this world without his permission, and that if God does not allow them to

Chapter five	Luis Santamaría del Río, in
	Ezenweke, Elizabeth Onyedinma (Ed.)
	Whose God Is God? Exploring The Concept Of God Within Religions
	London & Abuja, Adonis & Abbey Pulishers

come, they will not come" (p. 131). But this seems to be God's only activity; he does not intervene in the created world, but instead through the spirits who communicate with men.

Neopaganism: A Source and Element of NA

Before going on, it is necessary to point out that behind the important contributions of the esoteric world to the NA doctrine, the recovery of Pre-Christian Paganism in the configuration of some images of God in the NA is eminent. Neopaganism has also been integrated as an important element in the spiritual nebula of the NA, and every Neopagan branch includes its own gods and proposes its own pantheon. However, the key element that can be studied as an important source for the new religiosity is the role played by the Mother Goddess or the Feminine Deity.

Before studying the feminine Deity, it is necessary to point out the lack of doctrinal uniformity in the complex world of Neopaganism that is integrated by the most diverse spiritual traditions and modified same for the current world. Higginbotham (2008) explains that:

> Pagans usually approach the question of God with open-mindedness and flexibility.... Since there is no Pagan-wide dogma about Deity, there are no set or uniform opinions on the issue within Paganism as a whole. Most Pagans accept the likelihood that no two people will have exactly the same experiences of Deity.... Every discourse about God is reduced to ideas, to concepts, since there is no objective reality behind those words. It is, thus, a metaphorical language. This logically leads to a theological relativism. Pagans are not required, although they may so choose, to covenant with a particular Deity. They are free to hold whatever images of Deity that is meaningful to them. (pp. 75 - 76).

Invariably, adherents of this doctrine believe in many gods, although most seem to be essentially duotheistic, with just one God and one Goddess named and worshipped. Some groups are strictly monotheistic, worshiping the Goddess to the total exclusion of God. (Buckland, 2002).

The Deity in the Neopaganism is linked to nature, usually immanent to reality, which is also inside the person. Monaghan (1999) avers that:

> An immanent goddess does not exist outside the forms that embody her. These needs not to be human: many cultures have seen goddess energy as immanent in nature, with each plant having its own resident spirit who lives and dies with that tree or flower. (p. 9).

Unlike Christianity that is understood as a patriarchal religion, in the Neopagan spirituality, the feminine aspect prevails. Therefore, the ancient deities with female faces are recovered in a large variety of shapes. Reid-Bowen (2007) 0pines that "Some authors have coined the term 'Thealogy' as opposed to 'Theology' which is a form of radical feminist religious discourse that identifies itself as opposed to many of the male-identified discursive and methodological practices that have preceded it" (p. 6). In the most popular versions of all this doctrine, Pantheism is reached that widens the divinity from the Goddess to everything. In a very diffuse religiosity, specific of the NA, one can read, for instance, that "there are no rules to Goddess worship and no book of dogma. Whitworth succinctly observes that "Everything is sacred. Humans are not better than the rest of nature …. The self is celebrated, not denied. We are all goddesses and gods" (p. 114).

The Theorists and Promoters of the New Age

For a better understanding of the religiosity of the NA, we are going to directly study some of the main authors and representatives of the NA. It is also necessary to establish how all the discourse about God of this spirituality is a direct heir of the trends studied in detail above. First of all, the most representative authors of the NA thinkers will be studied, and then some samples of related literature will be analyzed. A good way to begin is by reference to *The Aquarian Conspiracy*, the main manifesto of the new spirituality, under the flag of a "paradigm shift" at several levels. Under the title "God within: the oldest heresy", Ferguson (1980) urges leaving behind the old concepts of Divinity and giving the name of God to the higher part of the universe. Continuing, Ferguson (1980) argues that:

> God is experienced as flow, wholeness, the infinite kaleidoscope of life and death, Ultimate Cause, the ground of being... God is the consciousness that manifests as Lila, the play of the universe. God is the organizing matrix we can experience but not tell, that which enlivens matter. (p. 382).

The Findhorn Foundation, in northern Scotland, cannot be forgotten when studying the NA's configuration. A perspective of the doctrine of its founders, the couple Eileen and Peter Caddy is useful to understanding the whole belief system of the new spirituality, which will be made more specific by some later authors. In her book *God spoke to me*, Caddy (1992) tells how in 1953 she heard an inner voice telling her to: "Be still and know that I am God. In stillness you find Truth. Find that secret place within yourself and in that place Truth will be revealed" (p. 107). It is a classical episode of revelation by means of channeling. That voice, low but firm, that inner source, was identified as "the God within". As her biographical book explains that:

> the messages received give her explicit directions for her life, making God's plan for her and her husband, Peter, clear in detailed guidance, and opening up for her and for others the greater dimensions and wonders of living in the New Age" (p. 11).

Therefore, this inner revelation experience can be seen to have foundational importance in terms of the NA theological thought.

Although it seems that she talks about a dialogue with that revelation source, one gets the impression when reading all her pages that there is a strong immanence, like when she asserts: "The truth shall set you free. You ask where you can find that truth. I tell you – deep within. Where can you find wisdom and understanding? Again I say 'within' (Caddy, 1992). This impersonal divinity manifested to Caddy is said to live in human bodies, which are his temples and that through them he reveals himself to the exterior, flowing like love energy. She indistinctly uses expressions applied in the Christian faith to the Father, the Son and the Holy Spirit, but here they are all written as if they had been said but by the same inner God. The truth, of Gnostic character, reveals itself in the inner part of the person, as it was already seen in the first quote. Of course, there is an essential unity of all these realities in the divinity. As it is stated, 'Behold the Oneness of your fellowmen in me; behold the perfection of my creation. In that risen state there is no darkness, no evil. All is one, all is united, and all is in me'. (Caddy, 1992).

Spangler (1988), an author who also belongs to the Findhorn Foundation, talks in similar terms to those already seen in Alice A. Bailey, when he states that "for God is both transcendent and immanent, beyond us and all with which we are familiar and still within us and our everyday world" (p. 41). According to this, the relation with God is, in the end, a perception of the divine in the own person. Mysticism is the experience of the wholeness in which we are embedded –the perception of the presence of God. It is an experience of unity with that presence, the discovery of the spirit of God within oneself. Mysticism shows us how we are one with God and co-participants with divinity in the enfoldment of creation. (Spangler, 1988).

This author contributes to the spiritual discourse of the NA with some interesting thoughts, when he asks himself about the legitimacy of jumping from considering the planet Earth as a living organism (as it happens in James Lovelock's "Gaia hypothesis") to her deification and adoration. Is it necessary to make nature sacred in order to preserve it? According to Spangler (1988), talking nowadays about the Goddess is more superficial and sentimental than spiritual. If the religious reference is serious, "invoking the spirit of Gaia is insufficient unless we understand just how we shape and participate in that spirit, and how we in turn are shaped and participated in by it."

The reflection, according to him, must be marked with ethical repercussions. This utilitarianism leads him to a negative answer when facing the attempt of the Earth deification: "We should not need to make either ourselves or the earth 'sacred' in order to love it and ourselves and to get on with doing what needs to be done to heal and

---

Chapter five | Luis Santamaría del Río, in
Ezenweke, Elizabeth Onyedinma (Ed.)
Whose God Is God? Exploring The Concept Of God Within Religions
London & Abuja, Adonis & Abbey Pulishers

protect the biosphere". He accepts the idea of Gaia, as a sort of enzyme or yeast that makes the conscience expands, catalyzing the process of human transformation. Based on his work, he concludes that we cannot *assume* the sacredness or spiritual livingness of the earth or accept it as a new ideology or as a sentimentally pleasing idea. We must experience that life and sacredness, if it is there, in relationship to our own and to that ultimate mystery we call God. (Spangler (1988).

Descending to the grounds of popular culture, one of the spiritual masters whose teachings are the most widely disseminated, Osho (2006), previously known as Bhagwan Shree Rajneesh and the representative of the Orientalism who transformed into a spiritual consumer product for the West, states a more diffuse concept of the Deity, which clearly leaves aside institutionalized religions as he vividly summed that:

> God is also wild, wilder than love. A civilized God is no God at all. The God of the church, the God of the temple is just an idol. God has disappeared from those places long ago, because God cannot be imprisoned. Those places are graveyards of God. If you want to find God, you will have to be available to the wild energy of life... God is the climax, the culmination, but God comes as a whirlwind. (p. 162).

This generalization, which is used to talk about God, reaches a clear Pantheism where the person identifies himself with the divine, as can be read in another of his books - In meditation you become God. People think in meditation they will see God. This is wrong; there is nobody to be seen. God is not an object. In meditation *you* become God –because all distinctions disappear. (Osho, 2006).

If we take a careful look at other less known authors, but who also sell many books and spread their doctrines through the different activities within the NA universe, the discourse is similar. The spokesperson of the advent of Maitreya, the Scottish writer Crème (1980) directly states that "Everything is God. There is nothing else in fact but God" (p. 103). The author of the famous book *A Course in Miracles*, Schucman (1975) says that "God is in everything I see" (p. 45), and also that "God is still everywhere and in everything forever.

And we are a part of Him" (p. 92) or that "there is no separation of God and His creation" (p. 136). Following this same line of thinking Walsch writes: "For God is the All, and the Goddess is everything, and there is nothing else that is" (p. 92).

At the beginning of his book, *Journey of a Soul*, John-Roger (2001), the founder of the Movement of Spiritual Inner Awareness, mixes up the idea of a creator God with the divine presence in everything existing and directly states that:

> The human being is a spark of that supreme reality: "In the beginning of time, God was in all places in an absolutely pure state. And in this purity, it was a void –without specific consciousness. In essence, God did not know itself, in awareness, in its greater beingness. So God instituted patterns of creation. It created universes, within which was what appeared to be solid objects (which we call planets) and less solid material (which we call space). All of it is God in Its different manifestations. And God instituted the plan that every part would know every other part –through experience. Thus the Soul, which is more directly the spark of God, was evolved and was given the opportunity to experience all levels, layers, planes and realms of experience and being.... The Soul that has experienced all is God and is one with God. (pp. 1-2).

In the work of John-Roger (2001) as cited above, one can observe how the man loses his personality when he merges with the Deity, in statements such as: "the Soul eventually dissolves its individuality into its greater oneness with the supreme God of all" (p. 5). Thus, human life is reduced to a path in the conscience of that great God formed by all. It is the nature of the Soul to experience all levels and conditions of God. Thus, the earth experience is part of the Soul's evolution into the greater consciousness of God. (John-Roger, 2001). In furtherance, John-Roger, (2001) concludes that "the divinity of the man is reasserted for we are each an extension of God and, as such, we have certain attributes in common with the one God." (p. 21).

Conclusive Thoughts

It is pertinent to take into account the fact that the NA is a heterogeneous thought system that is made up of many trends which do not share their main integral parts, despite that some authors have

Chapter five	Luis Santamaría del Río, in
	Ezenweke, Elizabeth Onyedinma (Ed.)
	Whose God Is God? Exploring The Concept Of God Within Religions
	London & Abuja, Adonis & Abbey Pulishers

made an inner typology that can be used for studying purposes. (Geoffroy, 1999). A common feature of all the studied models is the conscious distancing from all institutional and dogmatic conceptions of God, the explicit distancing from the theology of the Judeo-Christian sphere. The deity is not a strict object of faith or of systematic thought, but a personal experience. Therefore, the term "God" is used in many occasions to refer to the spiritual reality behind all reality or that which, in the end, confuses itself with it. As Hanegraaff (1998) explains, "this dimension, which is the guarantee for *meaning* is unproblematically treated as synonymous with God" (p. 183).

The second feature to be pointed out by the doctrines of the NA about God is his impersonal character, explained to a great extent by what has been mentioned before. Opposing a judging God imposed by traditional religions, a personal God who comes into relation with man, with supposedly negative features (father-patriarch, judge, punisher) and excessively anthropomorphic. The NA states the reality of a diffuse deity identified by positive human feelings; love, light, peace, energy, quiet, etc. To sum up, it does not matter how God 'is' but how I 'experience' God. There are some echoes of a apophatic theology when one talks about the deity so imprecisely; therefore, some authors like Hanegraaff (1998) have stated that "this vagueness is largely intentional, and results naturally from the belief that God's essence transcends the inherent limitations of human language and conceptual frameworks" (p. 186). In the end, there is no authorized word about this, falling into the most radical relativism; no one can say something about God that excludes the religious or spiritual experiences of anyone else.

This is linked to the question of communication between God and men. As it has already been pointed out in the examples quoted above, the deity reveals itself to man through what is real, and the most important place is the person's conscience. It is an intimate and individualist revelation or, as some authors have cleverly pointed out, a 'Self-Spirituality' (Aupers-Houtman, 2006) or a 'private symbolism' (Hanegraaff, 1999). It also has clear Gnostic features, because it is not

---

Chapter five | Luis Santamaría del Río, in
Ezenweke, Elizabeth Onyedinma (Ed.)
Whose God Is God? Exploring The Concept Of God Within Religions
London & Abuja, Adonis & Abbey Pulishers

a strictly believing relation where faith plays the key role, but knowledge and experience. In order to reach that knowledge and experience, the initiation, expansion, or elevation of the conscience is needed.

Pantheism or Panentheism are not fictitious risks, but real consequences of the NA doctrines about God, such as has been seen in the common pattern followed by the authors studied above. The echoes of some old thinking systems can be found in their beliefs, such as the conception of the Deity in Plato or the emanation of the One in Plotinus, as well as some elements of other monist or panentheist philosophical systems, like that one of Hegel. For this reason, some critics of the NA point out that the NA proposal is not new as its name portends, but brings back old conceptions and links these quoted philosophical systems with elements of the esoteric tradition, Orientalism, and pagan doctrines. All this is applied to their doctrine about God, as it has been analyzed in the present paper.

The NA defenders, in opposing the dualism that prevails in the contemporaneous Western culture, states that the unity of all reality; nature, humanity and God are, in their deepest essence, one. God is the source of being whose creative energy permeates and sustains all, and human beings are in their innermost being one with this source. When New Agers use the word *gnosis*, what they mean is precisely such a profound insight in the wholeness of reality, which overcomes alienation by reuniting the human individual with the All, or God. (Hanegraaff, 2007).

In fact, this Gnostic characterization of the NA is very important when valuing it and placing it in the current socioreligious context and in the history of religions. Because as the above-quoted expert acknowledges, "the New Age movement is evidently based on 'gnosis'; and this gnosis implies a rejection of at least one type of dualism discussed above; that is between human beings and God, creature and Creator. For gnosis in its traditional late-antique context likewise referred to the discovery that human beings are in their deepest essence one with divine reality (Hanegraaff, 2007). But, of course, the strong dualism characterizing old Gnosticism is rejected.

Chapter five	Luis Santamaría del Río, in
	Ezenweke, Elizabeth Onyedinma (Ed.)
	Whose God Is God? Exploring The Concept Of God Within Religions
	London & Abuja, Adonis & Abbey Pulishers

Furthermore, there is a trend to deify nature, as a reaction to the environment deterioration allegedly due to the distance established by the great monotheist religions between God and the created reality. As it has been recently pointed out (Santamaría, 2011), in the mixture appearing in the new religiosity of deep ecology, transpersonal psychology, and Neopaganism, an understanding of the world is created that elevates all the reality to the divine or energetic level. To sum up, it is a Pantheism that ends up reducing men to a shadow of a great universal mind, a cosmic conscience. Therefore, it is easy to understand the harsh criticism of the Christian Churches to the NA, criticism aiming at serious problems and anthropological risks in its spirituality. As Chryssides (2007) points out, "these include its panentheist tendencies and its location of divinity within the self, thus precluding notions of alterity, divine grace and sin" (p. 21).

References

Allen, A.L. (1914). *The Message of New Thought*. New York: Thomas Y. Crowell.

Atkinson, W.W. (2009, reprinted). *New Thought: Its History and Principles. The Message of The New Thought*. New York: Hudson Mohawk Press.

Atkinson, W.W. (2010, reprinted). *Law of the New Thought: A Study of Fundamental Principles and Their Application*. New York: Cosimo.

Aupers, S.D. – Houtman, D. (2006). Beyond the Spiritual Supermarket: The Social and Public Significance of New Age Spirituality. In *Journal of Contemporary Religion*, 21, 201-222.

Bailey, A.A. (1964). *Problems of Humanity*. New York: Lucis Trust.

Buckland, R. (2002). *The Witch Book. The Encyclopedia of Witchcraft, Wicca, and Neo-paganism*. Detroit: Visible Ink Press.

Caddy, E. (1992). *God Spoke to Me*. Moray: Findhorn Foundation.

Caddy, E. (1994). *The Spirit of Findhorn*. Forres: Findhorn Press.

Chryssides, G.D. (2007). Defining the New Age. In D. Kemp – J.R. Lewis, *Handbook of New Age* (pp. 5-24). Leiden: Brill.

Creme, B. (1980). *The Reappearance of the Christ and Masters of Wisdom.* Los Angeles: Tara Center.

Eddy, M.B. (1910). *Science and Health with Key to the Scriptures.* Boston: Mary Baker G. Eddy.

Ferguson, M. (1980). *The Aquarian Conspiracy. Personal and Social Transformation in the 1980s.* Los Angeles: J.P. Tarcher.

Fillmore, C. (1946). *Mysteries of John.* Kansas: Unity School of Christianity.

Geoffroy, M. (1999). Pour une typologie du nouvel âge. In *Cahiers de Recherche Sociologique*, 33, 51-83.

Grimassi, R. (2004). *Witchcraft: A Mistery Tradition.* St. Paul: Llewellyn Publications.

Guerra, M. (1998). *Diccionario enciclopédico de las sectas.* Madrid: Biblioteca de Autores Cristianos.

Hanegraaff, W.J. (1998). *New Age Religion and Western Culture: Esotericism in the Mirror of Secular Thought.* Albany: State University of New York Press.

Hanegraaff, W.J. (1999) New Age Spiritualities as Secular Religion: a Historian's Perspective. In *Social Compass*, 46, 145-160.

Hanegraaff, W.J. (2007) The New Age Movement and Western Esotericism. In D. Kemp – J.R. Lewis, *Handbook of New Age* (pp. 25-50). Leiden: Brill.

Higginbotham, J. & R. (2008). *Paganism: An Introduction to Earth-centered Religions.* Woodbury: Llewellyn Publications.

Holmes, E.S. (1926). *The Science of Mind. A Complete Course of Lessons in the Science of Mind and Spirit.* New York: R. M. McBride & Company.

Hunting, G. (1934). *Working with God.* Kansas: Unity School of Christianity.

Hutton, R. (1999). *The Triumph of the Moon: A History of Modern Pagan Witchcraft.* Oxford:Oxford University Press.

John-Roger (2001). *Journey of a Soul.* Los Angeles: Mandeville Press.

Kardec, A. (2006, reprinted). *The Spirits' Book.* New York: Cosimo.

Kardec, A. (2010). *What is Spiritism?* Brasilia: International Spiritist Council.

Lewis, J.R. (ed.). (2004). *The Encyclopedic Sourcebook of New Age Religions*. Amherst: Prometheus Books.

Monaghan, P. (1999). *The Goddess Path. Myths, Invocations & Rituals*. St. Paul: Llewellyn.

Mosley, G. (2006). *New Thought, Ancient Wisdom: The History and Future of the NewThought Movement*. West Conshohocken: Templeton Foundation Press.

Osho (2002). *Everyday Osho. 365 Daily Meditations for the Here and Now*. Gloucester: Fair Winds Press.

Osho (2006, reprinted). *Love and Meditation*. New Delhi: Diamond Pocket Books.

Partridge, C. (2007). Truth, Authority and Epistemological Individualism in New Age Thought. In D. Kemp – J.R. Lewis, *Handbook of New Age* (pp. 231-254). Leiden: Brill.

Peebles, J.M. (2003, reprinted). *What is Spiritualism*. Whitefish: Kessinger Publishing Co.

Ratzinger, J. (2004). *Truth and Tolerance: Christian Belief and World Religions*. San Francisco: Ignatius Press.

Reid-Bowen, P. (2007). *Goddess as Nature: Towards a Philosophical Thealogy*. Aldershot: Ashgate.

Santamaría, L. (2011). El hombre ante Gaia. La re-sacralización de la naturaleza en la Nueva Era. In J.R. Flecha Andrés (ed.), *Ecología y ecoética* (pp. 213-222). Salamanca: Universidad Pontificia de Salamanca.

Schucman, H. (1975). *A Course in Miracles*, Vols. 1-2. Tiburon: Foundation for Inner Peace.

Spangler, D. (1988). *Emergence: - The Rebirth of the Sacred*. London: Gateway Books.

Spangler, D. (1990). The Meaning of Gaia : Is Gaia a Goddess, or Just a Good Idea? *In Context. A Quarterly of Humane Sustainable Culture*, 24, 44 47. Available in http://www.context.org/ICLIB/IC24/Spangler.htm

Sutcliffe, S. (2007) The Origins of 'New Age' Religion Between the Two World Wars. In D. Kemp – J.R. Lewis, *Handbook of New Age* (pp. 51-75). Leiden: Brill.

Trine, R.W. (1910). *In tune with the Infinite.* New York: Dodge Publishing Company.

Walsch, N.D. (1997). *Conversations with God: An Uncommon Dialogue,* Book 2. Charlottesville: Hampton Roads.Whitworth, B. (2003). *New Age Encyclopedia.* Franklin Lakes: The Career Press.

CHAPTER SIX

God-Talk in Theistic Perspectives

Kanu, Ikechukwu Anthony (OSA) & Mgbemena, Stanley C.

Introduction

Generally, theism is based on the philosophy that the universe originates from a common source; as such, it maintains that the universe does not contain its own principles within itself. It encapsulates a body of religious faiths that includes: Judaism, Christianity and Islam. They all have a doctrine that avows that God created the world. In a broader sense, this piece understands theism as the belief in the existence of God. Having discussed the atheist's arguments against the existence of God in the previous chapter, this chapter is concern basically with the arguments of theists for the existence of God. Here, three arguments would take the centre stage: Teleological, Ontological and Cosmological arguments.

Teleological Argument

The word teleology is derived from two Greek words: *telos* meaning 'end or purpose' and *'logos'* meaning 'study or science'. Brought together, teleology would mean 'the science or end of purpose'. It has final causality as its synonym, and got her nuance in the 16th and 17th centuries with the development in the mechanistic approach of modern science; Averroes, the Islamic Philosopher, introduced teleological arguments in the Medieval Ages, when he said that people are inclined to infer the existence of a magnanimous creator from the magnificent design of the universe; Augustine had also argued that the universe is the effect of a cause, thus from creation, one can proceed to discover the creator; Thomas Aquinas employed this argument in fifth way, in which he speaks of the universe pointing to the creator. However, in the 18th century, teleology got a profound expression in the writings of William Paley (Kanu, 2012).

Chapter six	Kanu, Ikechukwu Anthony (OSA) & Mgbemena, Stanley C, in Ezenweke, Elizabeth Onyedinma (Ed.) *Whose God Is God? Exploring The Concept Of God Within Religions* London & Abuja, Adonis & Abbey Pulishers

William Paley (1743-1805)

He was an English theologian, born at Peterborough on July, 1743. His mother was a keen, thrifty woman of much intelligence, and his father was a minor canon at Peterborough. In 1758 Paley entered, as sizar, Christ College, Cambridge. He had been a fair scholar at his father's school, especially interested in mathematics. After taking his degree in 1763, he became an usher at an academy in Greenwich and, in 1766, was elected fellow of Christ College, where he became an intimate friend of John Law and lectured successfully on metaphysics, morals, and the Greek Testament. He had been ordained a priest in 1767, and was appointed to the rectory of Musgrave in Cumberland, which be resigned in 1776, to take the vicarage of the two parishes, Appleby and Dalston. In 1780, he was installed prebendary at Carlisle, and resigned Appleby on becoming archdeacon in 1782. At the close of 1785, he became chancellor of the diocese and (1789-92) figured as an active opponent of the slave-trade. In recognition of his apologetic writings, he was given the prebend of St. Pancras in St. Paul's Cathedral; the subdeanery of Lincoln, in 1795; and the rectory of Bishop Warmouth in 1795; and transferred his residence to Lincoln shortly before his death in 1805.

The Teleological Arguments of William Paley

There was never a time in the history of philosophy when teleological arguments regarding the existence of God received a powerful rhetorical formulation as in William Paley's analogy with a watch. He begins with the discovery of a watch, which when carefully examined, one will find out that the different parts fit and work together in an intricate manner. From this observation, the mind is led to infer that a designer or an intelligent agent is responsible for all that was discovered in the watch (Wainwright, 1989). In the case where the analogy of the watch is not plausible, he avers that one might consider the biological mechanism of living organisms. The design which is evident in the workability of living organisms suggests that a proportionately more intelligent being is responsible for such a design. The issue of proportionality is very strong in

Paley's argument, for it suggests that the more complex the design, the more complex the designer. However, the complexity of the design might go on, but very little is said about the designer. The idea of the designer in this case must be immaterial, for if it is material, it would be composed of parts, and would require that it is subject to another designer. The property of the designer as immaterial has a logic that helps us in knowing, at least, something about the designer, and annuls the problem of infinite regress.

David Hume criticised Paley's teleological arguments variously: as regards the idea of order in nature, Hume denies that there is order in the first place; he argues that it is rather something that human beings have imposed on the chaos of nature. And that even if there is order, the watch analogy is inappropriate, because of the interaction component parts of the watch is verifiable, while that of the universe is not. Presenting the problem of evil as a counter argument, Hume avers that if God is the creator of the universe and he is all good and perfect, it then means that the problem of evil, which is part of the universe, can also be traced back to its creator. He further argues that if the watch-universe only leads us to a designer, there is no proof that it is God.

The Ontological Arguments

The ontological (the science of being) argument for the existence of God is based entirely on reason. According to this argument, there is no need to go out looking for physical evidence of God's existence; we can work out that he exists by just thinking about it. Philosophers call such arguments *a priori* arguments.

Various philosophers have offered ontological arguments for the existence of God. However, it is traditional to focus in the first instance on the versions offered by St. Anselm, because he is best known in the history of philosophy to have conclusively and distinctively, proffered this argument.

Saint Anselm (c. 1033 – 1109)

This towering and complex figure has been described as the most luminous and penetrating intellect between St. Augustine and St. Thomas Aquinas. His early years gave little indication of his later achievements. Born into a land–owning family of Aosta in Lombardy (in present day northern Italy), he was a brilliant pupil but seems to have been persuaded by his father, Gundulf, to abandon the idea of a monastic calling and involve himself in worldly affairs, leading a life he later bitterly regretted as dissipated (Burns, 2007). But when his mother died he quarrelled with his father's family and left home at twenty three. After three years of apparently aimless travelling through Burgundy and France, he came to Normandy in 1059. Once in Normandy, Anselm's interest was captured by the Benedictine abbey at Bec, whose famous school was under the direction of Lanfranc, the Abbey's Prior.

In 1060 Anselm entered the abbey as a novice. His intellectual and spiritual gifts brought him rapid advancement, and when Lanfranc was appointed abbot of Caen in 1063, Anselm was elected to succeed him as prior. Subsequently, in 1078 he was elected abbot by a unanimous vote of the monks. This meant becoming a great temporal as well as spiritual lord, and Anselm was successful in expanding the abbey's lands and prestige while at the same time being a loving father to his monks (Burns, 2007). Under his leadership, the reputation of Bec as an intellectual centre grew, and Anselm managed to write a good deal of philosophy and theology in addition to his teaching, administrative duties, and extensive correspondence as an adviser and counsellor to rulers and nobles all over Europe and beyond. His works while at Bec include the *Monologion* (1075-1076), the *Proslogion* (1077-1078), and his four philosophical dialogues: *De Grammatico* (1059-1060), *De Veritate,* and *De Libertate,* and *De Casu Diaboli* (1080-1086).

Amidst political friction that existed between the Church and the government thereafter, Anselm refused to give in to the excessive and selfish demands of succeeding kings. Nevertheless, in 1093 Anselm was enthroned as Archbishop of Canterbury. The previous

Archbishop, Anselm's old master, had died four years earlier, but the king, William Rufus, had left the seat vacant in order to plunder the archiepiscopal revenues. Anselm was understandably reluctant to undertake the primacy of the Church of England under a ruler as ruthless and venal as William and his tenure as Archbishop proved to be as turbulent and vexatious as he must have feared. William was intent on maintaining royal authority over ecclesiastical affairs and would not be dictated to by Archbishop or Pope or anyone else. So, for example, when Anselm went to Rome in 1097 without the king's permission, William would not allow him to return. When William was killed in 1100, his successor, Henry I, invited Anselm to return to his seat. But Henry was as intent as William had been on maintaining royal jurisdiction over the Church, and Anselm found himself in exile again from 1103-1107.

Throughout his struggles, triumphs, and defeats he had been producing a stream of letters, devotional works, and, above all, the theological and philosophical treatises that were to earn him the title of Doctor of the Church. His guiding principle was the rule of St. Benedict; he lived in obedience to it and strove to create a community of love based on it, as prior and later abbot of Bec. His famous motto, *Fides Quaerens Intellectum* (Faith seeking understanding) underpinned his theological enquiries such as *Cur Deus Homo?* (Why did God become man?)

Anselm's Definition of God

Anselm defined God as 'that being than which none greater can be conceived'. He maintains that anyone who understands this definition has a conception of God in his understanding. Therefore God exists at least in his understanding. But it is possible for him to conceive of a being who exists not only in the understanding but in reality as well. This being, who resembles God in all other aspects, would thus be greater than the being who exists only in the understanding. But by definition, it is impossible to conceive of a being greater than God. God must therefore exist not only in the understanding but in reality as well. Thus, according to St. Anselm, from God's very definition, it follows that his nonexistence in reality is impossible, and therefore, that He must exist.

Following this definition, Anselm had tried to show that God's existence could be established solely from our knowledge of the concept 'God.' No other evidence is needed. The definition of the concept is such that the proposition 'God does not exist' must assert a logical contradiction (Avrum, 1969). Therefore, God necessarily exists!

Monologion

The *Monologion* (which contains his first treatise on the existence of God) was written at the request of the monks of Bec, where St. Anselm was Prior. His monks asked him to write a model meditation on God, in which everything would be proved by reason, with absolutely nothing depending on the authority of Scripture. This is surely a strange meditation for monks, but the request reflects the extraordinary interest at the time in rational speculation. Hence, in reply to his monk's demand St. Anselm sets out to give a rational proof of God's existence.

In the first part of the *Monologion* Anselm holds that degrees of perfection in things are basic pointers to a more superior and most perfect of all these things. For him, the various degrees of handsome men are basically pointers to an absolutely handsome reality. It is the same with various other qualities like goodness, gentleness, wisdom etc. They are all but limited manifestations of an absolute wisdom or goodness or any quality. St. Anselm holds that that absolute reality of all qualities is God. God is the supreme degree of all qualities. Any person or thing that holds any quality is merely a participant in this supreme quality rooted in God. Stressing this point further, he says we normally make degrees of comparisons which is the source of all and is God.

He clarifies this point with the quality of goodness when he argued that although we speak of things as being *good* in different degrees, these things must be good through some other thing. Clearly, that thing is itself a great good, since it is the source of the goodness of all other things. Moreover, that thing is good *through itself;* after all, if all good things are good through that thing, it follows trivially that that thing, being good, is good through itself. Things that are good through another (i.e. things whose goodness derives from something other than themselves) cannot be equal or greater than the good thing that is good through itself, and so that which is good through itself is supremely good.

Hence, all true good have the character of goodness through the same being, through which all good exists. This being is not good through something else; it is good through itself. Thus, it alone is supremely good, surpassing all others. It is indeed the most excellent of all beings; in a word, it is God! (Armand, 1969).

Using the same method, Anselm offers two more proofs of the existence of God. In the second, Anselm argues that all existing things exist through some one thing. Every existing thing, he begins, exists either through something or through nothing. But, of course, nothing exists through nothing, so every existing thing exists through something. Anselm (cited by Omoregbe, 2000), says:

> Whatever exists, either brought itself into existence or it was brought into existence by another being. But nothing can bring itself into existence, for that would involve a contradiction because it would have to exist because it would have to exist first before it can bring itself into existence. This is obviously a contradiction and impossible. Therefore, whatever exists was brought into existence by another being. Now, it is either the cause that existing beings brought each other into existence or one common being brought them all into existence. But it is impossible for beings to bring each other into existence. To say, for example, that A brought B into existence while B in turn also brought A into existence would be impossible. It follows, therefore, that a common being, only one being, brought all things into existence, and this being is God! (p. 79-80).

St Anselm's final argument is almost like a reformulation of the previous one. This is based on comparison. The fact that we compare things in terms of quality or perfection presupposes an absolute standard of perfection, and it is against the background of this absolute standard that comparison is made. To say, for example, that one thing is better than another means that it is nearer to the absolute standard of goodness than the other one.

For instance, a horse is better than wood, and a human being is more excellent than a horse. Now, it is absurd to think that there is no limit to how these levels can go, so that there is no level so high that an even higher level cannot be found. The only question is how many beings occupy that highest level of all. Is there just one, or are there more than one? Suppose there are more than one. By hypothesis, they must all be equals. If they are equals, they are equal through the same thing. That thing is either identical with them or distinct from them. If it is identical with them, then they are not, in fact, many, but one, since they are all identical with some one thing. On the other hand, if that thing is distinct from them, then they do not occupy the highest level after all. Instead, that thing is greater than they are, and this is God.

Proslogion

In the preface to the *Proslogion*, Anselm relates that after writing the *Monologion* he cast about in his mind for a simpler proof of God's existence. He then began by quoting the Psalmist in Psalm 14 vs. 1 and Psalm 53 vs. 1, Where it says: *The fool says in his heart; 'There is no God'!* St. Anselm wonders why the fool should say that there is no God, and he decided to prove to the fool that there is God.

He says that: although the fool has said that there is no God, when he hears of 'something than which nothing greater can be conceived', he understands what this means. This means that, although the fool denies that God ('that which nothing greater can be conceived') exists in reality, he cannot deny that God exists in the fool's mind or understanding. That is, the fool must have some idea of God in his mind in order to deny God's existence in reality, for if he did not have such an idea of God he would not know what he was talking about when he denies that that being exists in reality (Hamilton, 2003).

So, God exists in the mind or understanding – even in the mind or the understanding of the fool who denies that God exists in reality. Does God exist in any other way, or does he exist only in the understanding? Anselm says that if that than which nothing greater can be conceived exists *only in the understanding* then there is, after all something greater than that which nothing can be conceived. For if something exists in reality as well as in the understanding, then that thing is greater than the thing that exists only in the understanding.

Anselm then argues: it is absurd to suppose that there exists something greater than that which nothing greater can be conceived. For if there is something *greater* than that than which *nothing greater* can be conceived, then that than which nothing greater can be conceived is also *not* that than which nothing can be conceived. For example, when a painter thinks over in advance what he is going to paint, he has this in his intellect, but he is conscious that it does not yet exist in reality. But when he has painted it, he both has it in his intellect and understands that what he has produced really exists (Armand 1969).

Thus, in order to avoid this absurdity, we can conclude that, that than which nothing can be conceived must exist *in reality as well as in the understanding*. Therefore, that than which nothing greater can be conceived must exist in reality. But God is that than which nothing can be conceived. Therefore, God exists in reality. Therefore, God exists (Hamilton, 2003)!

More formally, the argument looks like this:

a. God, by the definition is the greatest being possible.
b. If God exists only in our minds, then it is possible for there to be a thing greater than God, namely a being like God that exists in reality.
c. But it is not possible to have a being greater than God.
d. Therefore God must exist in reality!

St. Anselm's proof has always found critics in philosophical circles. The first was one of his own contemporaries by the name of Gaunilon. This astute Benedictine monk from Marmoutier (Tours) wrote a remarkable pamphlet, "In Defense of the Fool", whom St, Anselm had said, could not really deny God's existence once he realized what the term God meant. Gaunilon's defenses consisted chiefly in arguing that if the ontological argument were valid, many strange conclusions would follow. Using the same type of reasoning, he contended, one could also show that an amazing variety of unreal or imaginary objects necessarily exists.

For instance, let us imagine a perfect island, an island than which no one greater can be conceived of. Although no explorer has yet found this island, it must exist according to St. Anselm's argument. If it does not exist, then it is not perfect (since it lacks the perfection existence.) And it is not that island than which none greater can be conceived of (since one can conceive of such an island as existing, a conception of a greater island than a nonexistent one.) Since, by definition, the island is perfect, and it is that island than which none greater can be conceived of. Its nonexistence is logically impossible. Hence from the concept alone, Gaunilon argued, it can be shown that a perfect island must necessarily exist in reality.

Gaunilon also sought to show that St. Anselm's ontological argument was absurd, in that, if valid, it would lead to ridiculous conclusions. It would, he argued, establish that a perfect island must exist. St. Anselm replied that these absurd conclusions would not follow, since the ontological argument could be applied *only* to the being than which a greater cannot be thought, (which is God) and not to any other thing. Hence, St. Anselm insisted there could be no other being than whose essence entails his existence (Avrum, 1969).

Another proponent of the ontological arguement is Rene Descartes (1596 – 1650.) He defined God as the most perfect being possible instead of the greatest being possible. The most perfect being possible possesses all possible perfections. Because existence is a perfection (it's better to exist than not to exist), God exists. Here's how Descartes (1911) puts it:

> Whenever I choose to think of the first and supreme being and as it were bring out the idea of him from the treasury of my mind, I must necessarily ascribe to him all perfections, even if I do not at the moment enumerate them all, or attend to each. This necessity clearly ensures that when later on I observe that existence is a perfection, I am justified in concluding that the First and Supreme Being exists (p. 187).

Chapter six | Kanu, Ikechukwu Anthony (OSA) & Mgbemena, Stanley C , in Ezenweke, Elizabeth Onyedinma (Ed.)
Whose God Is God? Exploring The Concept Of God Within Religions
London & Abuja, Adonis & Abbey Pulishers

Hence, his arguements can be put this way :

a. God, by definition, possesses all possible perfections.
b. Existence is a perfection.
c. Therefore, God exists!

In each of these versions of the ontological arguement, the basic contention is that the definition of God is such that His existence is part of his nature and essence. Hence, it is a logical consequence of the definition that God exists. For Anselm, Descartes and Spinoza, what differentiated the concept of God from all others was that His was the only one which necessarily entailed existence. The definition of any other entity allows for the possibility that the entity may or may not exist. Only God's Essence logically implies his existence. Thus, only God's existence can be established *a priori*, from the concept alone, without any reference at all to any facts about the world.

The Cosmological Arguments

The cosmological argument was properly systematized by St. Thomas Aquinas in his Five Ways of proving the existence of God .The proof begins from concrete, existing realities. Hence, he contended that it is possible to gain knowledge about the nature and existence of God, but that this could not be accomplished by purely *a priori* reasoning. The procedure must be from the known to the unknown; we must start our argument from the things that are seen around us. The proof is in three species. Each traces the origin of things at the backdrop of the principle of causality: Cause of movements (proof from Motion); Efficient cause of being (proof from Efficient Causality); and Necessary cause (proof from Necessity and Contingency). At the end of each explanatory chain, we arrive at a Supreme or Final Cause, what we call God (Aquinas, 1948).

Saint Thomas Aquinas (c.1225 – 1274)

This great Medieval theologian and philosopher was born mid-way between Rome and Naples near the small town of Aquino, of which his father was count and his mother, a noblewoman. He started his schooling at the age of five, at the nearby Benedictine abbey of Monte Cassino. There, he received his elementary education from a Benedictine monk. But political turmoil broke out and he was sent to the University of Naples at the age of twelve, where he was introduced to the works of Aristotle.

At Naples, he was drawn to the Dominican order, founded twenty years earlier, largely on account of the scholarship its members were already demonstrating in University circles, and because he was attracted by their ideals of poverty, preaching and teaching. Despite being locked in a castle and tempted with a courtesan by his parents, he joined the order in 1224. He studied under Albert the great, first at Paris and then at Cologne. He was ordained a priest during his time at Cologne, where Albert prophesied that "the lowing of this dumb ox" – Thomas was physically large and spoke little – "would be heard all over the world" (Albert cited by Burns 2007).

He was appointed to a lectureship in Paris in 1252, and four years later, at the early age of thirty-one, he was made a master of theology, which imposed the threefold task of lecturing, disputing, and preaching. He encountered quite ferocious opposition, mainly from the leader of the secular clergy, William of Saint-Amour, who saw the mendicant orders and their poverty as heralding the arrival of the anti-Christ. Before he left Paris, Thomas began work on one of his main works titled, *Summa Contra Gentiles*.

In 1259 Aquinas returned to his homeland, Italy, where he taught at several places, including Orvieto, Viterbo, and Rome, for the next ten years. He also traveled to various cities in fulfillment of duties in connection with his order and the Papal court. He continued to preach, teach and write. Thus, he was able to finish the *Summa Contra Gentiles* and to start his great literary work *Summa Theologica*, besides composing a number of smaller books. However, it must be noted

---

Chapter six | Kanu, Ikechukwu Anthony (OSA) & Mgbemena, Stanley C , in Ezenweke, Elizabeth Onyedinma (Ed.)
Whose God Is God? Exploring The Concept Of God Within Religions
London & Abuja, Adonis & Abbey Pulishers

that his writings are too extensive in number, scope, and achievement to be presented here in any meaningful summary (Burns 2007).

All this time, the Church offered to make him Archbishop of Naples and abbot of Monte Cassino, but he refused both. He preferred to remain a Dominican Friar, practicing extraordinary acts of penance, sensational deeds and mortifications. Thomas had been a pure person, humble, simple, peace-loving, given to contemplation, moderate, and a lover of poetry. His manners showed his breeding, for people described him as refined, affable and lovable. In arguments, he maintained self control and won over his opponents by his personality and great learning.

The Dominicans recalled him to Italy in 1272 to re-organize their house of studies at Naples. He remained there until 1274 when he was summoned by Pope Gregory X to take part in the Council of Lyons. Thus, he set out on what would have been a long and arduous journey, but after only a few hours he suffered a major stroke. He was taken to the castle of Maenza, which belonged to a niece, and then at his request transferred to the Monastery of Fossanuova, where he died on 7th March 1274, leaving a body of work that would have taken three normal lifetimes to compose (Burns 2007).

He was canonized in 1323 by Pope John XXII. He was highly praised at the Council of Trent, and in 1567 the Dominican Pope St. Pius V declared him Doctor of the Church, and he is generally known as 'Doctor *Angelicus*', 'Doctor *Universalis*' and 'Doctor *Communis*'. He was the foremost classical proponent of natural theology, and the father of the Thomistic school of philosophy and theology. He is the patron saint of Catholic Schools, Colleges and Universities, of their teachers and students and, by extension, of education in general.

The Five Ways

Aquinas believed that the existence of God is neither self-evident nor beyond proof. In the *Summa Theologica*, he considered in great detail five rational proofs for the existence of God. These are widely known as *quinquae viae*, or the "Five Ways". These proofs are not original; each can be traced back to the philosophers of antiquity or the middle ages. But in his hands they are transformed and lead to the existence, not of the God of Aristotle or the Arabian philosophers, but of the God of Christianity (Armand, 1968).

Since the five ways are found in a treatise that is theological, and not philosophical, to expect the proofs as given in the *Summa* by St. Thomas to expound the full metaphysical implications would be to confuse theology with philosophy. Yet, the five ways are truly proofs; "way" is not meant to indicate some weak expression, but rather the strong work of the theologian in his rational approach (Smith 2003).

Proof from Motion

The first and most evident way of proving God's existence is from motion. It is certain, and evident on the basis of sense experience that some things are in motion. Nothing moves unless it is acted upon by something else, that is, unless its potentiality is actualized by some entity already in a state of actuality. Nothing can move itself, since it would have to be actual and potential in the same respect at the same time (Avrum 1969). For motion is nothing else than the reduction of something from potentiality to actuality. Hence, a being cannot be brought from potentiality to actuality except by a being in act.

In the example St. Thomas Aquinas used, something such as wood is moved to become hot only by something that is already hot, such as fire. An object cannot make itself hot, for it then would have to be hot and not hot simultaneously. At first sight, the self movements of living beings seem to be an exception to this rule, but on closer examination we see that they have parts, on which moves the other (Armand, 1968).

Thus, whatever is moved must be moved by something other than itself. The mover must also by the same reasoning, be moved by some other mover, and so on. The sequence of movers and motions cannot go back infinitely, because if there is no first mover, there can be no second, no third, and so on. Hence, there could be no present motion, which is contrary to our experience. Therefore, it is necessary to arrive at a first mover, moved by no other (unmoved mover) who is not subject to change, but who is the source of all motion; and this everyone understands to be God (Avrum, 1969).

Some scholars have said that this argument is weak because it is false, that nothing can change itself or move itself. Cannot people and animals do this all the time? But Thomas does not mean to deny that animals and people can move themselves at will, for example. His point can be seen if we consider an example. Suppose I open my mouth to speak. Then I have changed. But how have I done this? I can only start speaking by virtue of my not having been speaking up to the moment when I begin to do so. Hence, there must be some aspect of me that brings about the speaking. In other words, some part of me causes another part of me to do something. In this sense, I do not cause myself to speak, and indeed, generalizing, we can say that nothing changes itself (Hamilton, 2003).

Proof from Efficient Cause

Aquinas' second argument is based on efficient causality. It is very similar to the first argument and follows the same process. In the world of sensible things, says Aquinas, we find there is an order of efficient causes. We know that nothing can be the cause of itself. Rather, we find that one thing is the cause of another thing, and that which is the cause of another is itself also caused by something else, and so on.

For example, the wind causes the leaves to fall off the tree. Each cause itself is caused. Nothing ever causes itself, for a cause always precedes its effect, and for something to cause itself it would have to precede itself. This, then, shows that there is a chain or series of causes in the universe. If we continue tracing causes, we cannot go on *ad infinitum*. We are bound to come to the first cause, the very beginning of the series of causes. Aquinas (cited by Omoregbe, 2000), therefore says that 'it is necessary to admit a first efficient cause, to which everyone gives the name of God' (p. 86).

To say that God is the first mover or cause, is not to say that God is such a cause in a temporal or chronological sense. Thomas is not thinking of a long series of causes stretching back in time with God at the beginning, that is, of what one might call a 'horizontal' chain of causes. He could not be thinking of this, for that might make his argument absurd. The absurdity would be that he would then be saying that everything is caused by something else and then conclude that there is an exception to this, namely God. The conclusion of the argument would, therefore, contradict one of the premises. What Thomas has in mind is something else. He is thinking of a first cause that operates *here and now* to sustain a given causal chain in existence (Hamilton, 2003).

Proof from Contingency of Finite Beings

The third proof is a little more complex. It proceeds from the fact that, we find in the natural world that it is possible for objects to be or not to be. The fact that objects are generated, and that they degenerate shows that it is possible for them to exist and also to be nonexistent. The fact that they come into existence shows that it is possible for them to be and for them not to have been. It is not possible for objects that can exist or not exist to remain in existence forever, or to have been existing forever. Hence, the things that we see around us exist contingently. That is, although they exist, their non- existence is possible. Contingently, existing things might not have existed. For example, the plants in the garden exist, but they might not have, for they might not have been planted in the first place, or they might not have grown through a lack of rain.

St. Thomas maintains that if everything cannot-be, then at one time there was nothing in existence. Assuming that the world has been going on for an indefinite length of time, there must have been a time before each object came into being, and hence a time when it was not. If each object is only possible, then there must have been a time when *none* of the objects existed. If this state of affairs had ever occurred, there would now be nothing in the world, because the things in the world would have had to be brought into existence by something else. If there really was nothing in the world at some time, no things could be produced thereafter. Since it is obvious that there is, in fact, something in the world, it could never have been the case that all things were once nonexistent, nor, therefore, that all the things in the world are only possible.

Thus, something in the world must have a necessary and not just a possible existence (otherwise everything would have been nonexistent at some point in time). Its necessity must in turn be caused by something else that also exists necessarily. For the same reason that there cannot be an infinite regress of efficient causes, there cannot be an infinite regress of necessary causes of the necessary existence of certain things. Therefore, we have to admit that there must be some being which is the cause of its own necessary existence, and which causes the necessary existence of other beings. This all men speak of as God (Avrum 1969).

Proof from Grades of Perfection

The fourth argument is based on the various grades of perfection in things. Among beings there are some more and some less good, true, noble, and the like. Hence, we notice that things differ in quality: one thing is better than another, another one is found to be better even than the previous one, and later we find another that is better even than this very one, and so on. This is true as regards all qualities – beauty, goodness, justice, power, etc. When we compare things in terms of quality, we are measuring them with an absolute standard, the highest standard of perfection. This, Aquinas says, is the maximum perfection (Omoregbe, 2000).

This 'Maximum' is the cause of the being of all other beings, and the qualities we find in them in various degrees. Following Aristotle, Aquinas says that as fire which is the maximum heat is the cause of all hot things, so is the 'maximum' the cause of all beings and all their qualities. Hence, every good thing is the result of what is best, insofar as what is best provides the basis for assessing the goodness of everything else. Therefore, there must be something truest, best and noblest and consequently being in the highest degree. This noblest and most perfect being, which is the cause of all other beings with their relative perfections, we call God (Armand 1968).

Chapter six | Kanu, Ikechukwu Anthony (OSA) & Mgbemena, Stanley C , in
Ezenweke, Elizabeth Onyedinma (Ed.)
Whose God Is God? Exploring The Concept Of God Within Religions
London & Abuja, Adonis & Abbey Pulishers

Proof from Order

The fifth and final argument of Aquinas is based on teleology or order observable in nature. He says that we see that things which lack knowledge, such as natural bodies, act for an end, and this is evident from their acting always in the same way so as to obtain the best result. Aquinas' point is that non-rational beings seem to be acting for specific ends or pursuing certain goals. But we know that as non-rational beings they cannot be acting like this on their own initiative because, whatever lacks knowledge cannot move towards an end, unless it be directed by some being endowed with knowledge and intelligence.

In the overwhelming majority of cases, the earth brings forth her fruits and is thoroughly predictable as to her activities. Although lacking knowledge, the acorn is moved almost without exception towards its proper end of becoming an oak. Such uniform and consistent attainment of goals by nescient beings requires an explanation. To attribute it all to *chance* would be hopelessly naïve, since chance by its own connotation means something out of the ordinary, something not within the normal order of procedure. A more profound explanation must be sought.

St. Thomas's example, chosen with his customary precision, is that of an arrow moving toward a target. The arrow is directed towards its end; so is nature. The arrow depends entirely on the archer for its operation; nature depends entirely on something outside herself. Lack of knowledge is a definite limitation in a being acting for an end; the lack must be supplied in some way from without, by a knowing being.

Thus, the orderly movement of natural things towards their proper ends indicates the presence of an intelligent being. Order demands intelligence, because order is the arrangement of things in a definite series according to a norm, and only an intellect can conceive the relationships involved in such arrangement. The establishment of means to an end requires some foresight, some comprehension of relations, and even more primary, a conception of the end itself. Only an intelligent being satisfies these conditions.

Chapter six	Kanu, Ikechukwu Anthony (OSA) & Mgbemena, Stanley C, in Ezenweke, Elizabeth Onyedinma (Ed.) *Whose God Is God? Exploring The Concept Of God Within Religions* London & Abuja, Adonis & Abbey Pulishers

However, there are numerous cases in which natural things fail to attain their end, but the failure is due to what may be called accidental interference; thus the acorn will die in the earth if conditions for its survival are not present. At any rate, instances of failure can never outweigh the overwhelming evidence that exists for order and finality. The fact that nature does consistently attain her goals argues to the existence of an intelligent being. Furthermore, the constant achievement of the end means that the intellect responsible for the operations is never idle, but is exercising its causality continuously. And the intelligent ruler who exercises universal and constant direction over nature is the being men call God.

Much confusion over the fifth way is avoided if one remembers that the demonstration is concerned only with internal finality, not with external finality. An acorn is of its own intrinsic nature, potentially, an oak tree; it has a tendency to attain that end in a favourable environment. Later, the tree may be chopped down and made into toothpicks; but that involves another scheme of things not pertinent to the fifth way. Hence, the answer to the question whether the purpose or end of the egg is to be a chicken or an egg sandwich is: the intrinsic end of the egg is to be a chicken; the external ends of the egg are as limitless as its possibilities (Smith 2003).

As we end these five proofs for the existence of God, it is pertinent to note that, each of these proofs, St. Thomas contended, starts from an obvious and indisputable fact of human experience. The examination and understanding of the facts, in terms of Aristotle's philosophy, leads by five different paths to the conclusion that a certain kind of being exists, whom men call "God". We gain the knowledge that God exists by natural and rational means, seeking to find the necessary and sufficient reason for certain facts. This is the knowledge that God is!

Evaluation and Conclusion

Theism does not perfectly explain the existence of God. But, this inability to perfectly or convincingly explain the concept of God is not in any way contradicting the proposition that: God exists! And, of course, no objective mind would seek for perfection in our imperfect world. For example, in St. Thomas Aquinas' argument from motion, we could criticize him saying that: motion cannot be traced beyond the universe to a being outside it. If we say that there is a chain or series of movers in the universe and we trace this series to God as the last in the series, it means that God is part of the series and is, therefore, part of the universe. This argument, therefore, makes God part of the universe since he is seen as one of the series of movers in the universe.

Also, in the proof from grades of perfection, we could also say that the argument is weak because it makes God the best thing, that is, the best among things. This obviously reduces God to the level of a *thing*. For the best of all things, in spite of its being the best still remains a thing. However, in all these, it must be noted that both St. Anselm and St. Thomas Aquinas did not in any way contradict their earlier proposition that God exists. The only weakness that could be found in their proof is the limitation of using human language in explaining divine concepts or attributes.

In The argument of Bertrand Russell who replied that there is not enough evidence to believe in God, one might be forced to ask him: Are there really no evidence to prove God's existence? However, Edwards (Cited by Aliba, 2008), the great 18th century American theologian refutes this claim saying that while every human being has been granted the capacity to know God, successful use of these capacities require an attitude of "True benevolence", a willingness to be open to the truth about God. Thus, the failure of non-believers to see "divine things" is due to a dreadful stupidity of mind, occasioning an insensibility to their truth and importance.

Finally, as Leibniz (cited by Aliba, 2008) puts it: "Try as we may, we cannot do without God." This is a reality both theoretically and practically. Practically, all through history, over ninety-nine percent of humanity has, via different religions, held tenaciously to God as explanatory of their existence and the existence of all other realities outside God. Theoretically, all have been involved. Positively involved are those who, having accepted the reality of God by faith or

---

Chapter six | Kanu, Ikechukwu Anthony (OSA) & Mgbemena, Stanley C, in Ezenweke, Elizabeth Onyedinma (Ed.)
Whose God Is God? Exploring The Concept Of God Within Religions
London & Abuja, Adonis & Abbey Pulishers

(in) direct religious and other life experience, either try to demonstrate rationally his existence, nature and attributes, or do not see the need for such demonstrations as their faith-convictions suffice for them. Involved also, but negatively, are the meager fraction of humanity who tacitly, overtly, theoretically or existentially try to or actually do deny this reality of God's existence (Iroegbu 1995).

When in 1948, Bertrand Russell and Fredrick Copleston went on U.S television to debate on the existence of God, both (one theist, the other agnostic) did agree on one understanding (in other words, one definition) of God as: "A supreme personal being- distinct from the world and creator of the world" (Iroegbu, p. 133).

However, it must be noted that Atheism serves to caution religions to reasonable application of terminologies to metaphysical beings. Since it is necessary for man to believe in the true God, the task is, therefore, placed before all religions to justify their theistic claims with intelligent and convincing arguments. God should no longer be clothed in mythological garments that completely shade off his essential nature, and thereby giving birth to more hardened atheists who are not willing to compromise scientific clarity with religious obscurity.

Hence, this is also a clarion call to all adherents of religion to begin to live up to the expectation of reconciling their religious beliefs (profession of faith) with their actions. This is because; some adherents of religion do not live what they preach. Rather, they preach that God exists, but they live as though He does not exist. Who knows, when they begin to live according to their creed, many atheists will come to be converted into really believing that there is a God.

However, if contemporary atheism refuses to accept the metaphysical order, the sphere in which God reigns, a great injury will have been done the human person who is psychosomatically composed. Paradoxically, the atheists do not appear to know that their philosophical absolutisation of scientific method is just a means by which they try to get as near as possible to the supreme ideal. The occasional inadequacies and failures of these scientific methods already postulate an ideal that has not been achieved, at least in full. Religion has not, therefore, erred in its doctrine of hope, and man must continue to hope in God who necessarily exists outside of this finite order. In this light, atheism in whatever form can be seen for what it really is, namely a dangerous phenomenon that cuts man off from his rightful source of being. In other words, wise people will still seek God whom they know and believe to really exist (Elue, 2002).

References

Aliba, S. (2008).
Aquinas, T. (2008). *Summa Theologiae.* Maryland: Christian Classics.
Armand, M. (1968). *Medieval Philosophy.* New York: Random House.
Avrum, S. & Popkin, R. (1969). *Introduction to Philosophy.* New York: Holt, Rinehart and Winston.
Burns, P. (2007). *Butler's Saint for the Day.* London: Burns and Oates.
Descartes, R. (1911). 'Meditation V', *The Philosophical Works of Descartes,* trans. E.S. Haldane and G. R. T. Ross. Cambridge: Cambridge University Press.
Elue, M.O. (2002). The Fool Says in his Heart there is no God. *WAJOPS, 5. 76.*
Hamilton, C. (2003). *Understanding Philosophy.* Cheltenham: Nelson Thornes.
Iroegbu, P. (1995). *Metaphysics: The kpim of Philosophy.* Owerri: International
 Universities Press.
Kanu, I. A. (2012). *Theist's Arguments for the Existence of God.* Lecture note, St Augustine's Major Seminary, Jos.
Omoregbe, J. (2000). *A Philosophical Look at Religion.* Ikeja: Joja Educational Research and Publishers.
Smith, R.C. (2003). God, Proofs for the Existence of God. In *New Catholic Encyclopedia.* 2nd edition. Vol.6. Detroit: Gale Group.

CHAPTER SEVEN

God in African Traditional Religion

Ezenweke, Elizabeth Onyedinma

Background.

In the discussion of the issue of God in Africa, a clarification of the element of nomenclature needs to be made. There are basically two schools of thought on whether the religious nature of Africans should be named African Traditional Religion as propagated by E. Idowu (Idowu, 1973) or African Traditional Religions as proposed by J.S. Mbiti. In any case, it is a common thought that though Africa consists of thousands of smallscale societies who have distinct languages, kinship, systems, mythologies, ancestral memories, and homelands. These different societies comprise more than 200 million people throughout the planet today, yet, as J.V. Taylor corroborates, there is a remarkable number of features as well as the fact of a basic worldview which fundamentally is everywhere the same in sub-Saharan Africa. For instance, central to indigenous traditions is an awareness of the integral and whole relationship of symbolic and material life. Ritual practices and the cosmological ideas which under gird society cannot be separated out as an institutionalized religion from the daily round of subsistence practices. Cosmologies, or oral narrative stories, transmit the worldview values of the people and describe the web of human activities within the powerful spirit world of the local bioregion.

Thus, African traditional religion refers to the entire system of belief of the Africans before it came in contact with external influence. It is the indigenous religion of the Africans as conditioned by the geographical, social, economic and political factors of Africa.

God has long been acknowledged to be at the center of African life and institutions ever before the birth and existence of man. Before Africa came into contact with any form of civilization, she sought, knew and comprehended God. Based on insufficient knowledge of the philosophy underlining African belief system coupled with superiority complex, what these missionary witnessed were apparently very much unlike the religious forms they were familiar with in their respective homelands. They had not witnessed religious temples, churches or mosques. This hitherto, raised some serious doubt amongst them whether indigenous Africans had any knowledge of God. They, however, described African belief system with various derogatory terms such as barbaric, paganism, and uncivilized. No wonder Parrinder (1977), quoting the derogatory statement of Ludwig who asked 'How can the untutored African conceive God?' (P.9).

Notwithstanding the biased mindset towards the African culture by the early missionaries, Africans have a comprehensive knowledge of God. They are notoriously religious and each people has its own religious system, beliefs and practices. (Mbiti, 1969). The central essence of the religious life of the traditional Africa is the notion of a supersensible God that is known by various names by the various ethnic groups in Africa. (Karade, 1994). These names as originally compiled by Prof John S. Mbiti and tabulated herein are as shown below:

African Names For God:

AFRICAN PEOPLES AND THEIR NAMES FOR GOD
Originally compiled by Prof. John Mbiti and tabulated by Dr.Elizabeth Ezenweke

COUNTRY	TRIBE	NAMES FOR GOD
Angola	BACONGO	Nzambi
Angola	LUIMBE	Nzambi, Kalunga
Angola	OVIMBUNDU	Suku, Usovoli
Angola	Chokwe	Kalunga, Zambi

Chapter seven | Ezenweke, Elizabeth Onyedinma, in
Ezenweke, Elizabeth Onyedinma (Ed.)
Whose God Is God? Exploring The Concept Of God Within Religions
London & Abuja, Adonis & Abbey Pulishers

Angola	LUNDA-LUENA	Nzambi, Kalunga, Sakatanga
Benin	EWE	Mawu
Benin	Fon	Mawu-Lisa
Benin	Twi	Onyankopon
Botswana	SAN	Urezhwa
Botswana	Tswana	Modimo
Botswana	BAKWENA-TSWANA	Modimo
Burkina Faso	DOGON	Amma
Burkina Faso	LODAGAA	Na'angmin
Burkina Faso	Mossi	Winnam, Ouennam, Winde, Naba Zidiwinde
Burkina Faso	Tallenzi	We, Wene, Nawe, Nabwe
Burkina Faso	MOSSI	Winnam, Ouennam, Winde, Naba Zidiwinde
Burundi	Barundi	Imana, Rangicavyose, Rugiravyose, Indavyi, Rurema, Rugoba, Haragakiza, Harerimana, Rutunga, Rutangaboro, Segaba, Umusemyi, Mushoborave, Nyeninganyi, Rushoboravo, Ntakimunani, Inchanyi, Ruremabiboo, Rufashaboro, Ntirandekuva,

Cameroon	Bamileke	Si
Cameroon	Bamum	Njinyi or Nui, Yorubang
Cameroon	Balu	Mebee
Cameroon	Duala	Loba, Owasi, Iwonde, Ebasi
Cameroon	Balu	Mebee
	EKOI	Osawa, Nsi
Cameroon	Fang	Nzeme
Cameroon	Kpe	Lova or Loba
Cameroon	NSÓ	Nyuẏ
Cameroon	Tikar	Nyooiy
Central African Republic	BAYA	So, Zambi
Congo	BACHWA	Djakomba, Djabi
Congo	Balese	Katshonde, Tole, Mongo, Mbali, Londi
Congo	Baluba	Leza, Lesa-Waba
Congo	Bambuti	Arebati, Epilipili, Baatsi
Congo	Banen	Hoel, Kolo, Ombang
Congo	Alur	Jok, Jok Rubanga, Jok Nyakaswiya, Jok Odudu, Jok Adranga, Jok Atar
Congo	KUBA	Nceme, Mbombo, Njambe
Congo	Lele	Njambi
Congo	Lendu	Gindri
Congo	Logo	Tore, Ore, Ori, Djuka
Congo	Lugbara	Adroa or Adronga, Adro
Congo	Mamvu-Mangutu	Mai, Oti, Tore, Kundumbendu, Oto
Congo	Ngome	Akongo, Bilikonda, Ebangala, Ebangala-e-mokonda, Eliamokonda, Eli*Mali*ma, Endandala
Congo	Pygmy	Kmvoum

Chapter seven	Ezenweke, Elizabeth Onyedinma, in Ezenweke, Elizabeth Onyedinma (Ed.) *Whose God Is God? Exploring The Concept Of God Within Religions* London & Abuja, Adonis & Abbey Pulishers

Congo	Sonata	Nja
Congo	Vili	Nzambi, Mpungu
Congo	Nkundo	Djakomba
Congo	Lunda-Luena	Nzambi, Kalunga, Sakatanga
Côte d'Ivoire	Adjuru	Nyam
Côte d'Ivoire	Asante	Nyame, Onyankopon, Bore-Bore, Otumfoo, Otomankoma, Ananse Kokroko, Onyankopon Kwame
Côted'Ivoie	Lobi	Tangba You
Equatorial Guinea		
Ethiopia	Boran	Waqa
Ethiopia	Burji-Konso	Illalei, Bambelle
Ethiopia	Burji-Konso	Illalei, Bambelle,
Ethiopia	Gelaba	Yer
Ethiopia	Gofa	Tsuossa
Ethiopia	Gumuz	Robboqua, Fogatza, Musa, Musa Gueza
Ethiopia	Hadya	Wa'a
Ethiopia	Ingassana	Tie
Ethiopia	KAFA	Yaro
Ethiopia	Kemant	Sanbat
Ethiopia	Koma	Yere Siezi, War, Wal
Ethiopia	Konso	Bamballe, Adota, Waq
Ethiopia	Kuca	Tosso
Ethiopia	Kullo	Tosa
Ethiopia	Male	Sosi
Ethiopia	Mao	Yere, Yeretsi
Ethiopia	Masongo	Waqaio
Ethiopia	Mekan	Tuma
Ethiopia	Murle	Tummu

Ethiopia	Oromo	Waqa
Ethiopia	Sangama	Zabi
Ethiopia	Udhuk	Arumgimis
Ethiopia	Walamo	Tosa
Ethiopia	Zala	Taosa
Gabon		
Gambia		
Ghana	Asante	Nyame, Onyankopon, Bore-Bore, Otumfoo, Otomankoma, Ananse Kokroko, Onyankopon Kwame
Ghana	Akan	Nyame, Nana Nyankopon, Onyame, Amowia, Amosu, Amaomee, Totorobonsu, Brekyirihunuade, Abommubuwafre, Nyaamanekose, Tetekwaframua, Nana, Borebore
Ghana	Fanti	Nyame, Nyankopon
Ghana	Ga	Dzemawon, Numbo
Ghana	Konkomba	Omborr
Ghana	Lodagaa	Na'angmin
Ghana	Tallenzi	We, Wene, Nawe, Nabwe
Ghana	Twi	Onyankopon
Ghana	Birifor	We, Nawe, Wene, Yini
Ghana	Grunshi	We
Gambia	Serer	Rog
Guinea	Kissi	Hala
Guinea	Mdinge	Gala, Guele, Jalang
Guinea	Tenda	Hounounga
Ivory Coast	Ebrie	Nyangka
Ivory Coast	Lobi	Tagba You
Kenya	Abaluyia	Wele, Nyasaye, Nabongo, Khakaba, Isaywa

Chapter seven	Ezenweke, Elizabeth Onyedinma, in Ezenweke, Elizabeth Onyedinma (Ed.) *Whose God Is God? Exploring The Concept Of God Within Religions* London & Abuja, Adonis & Abbey Pulishers

Kenya	Akamba	Mulungu, Ngai, Mumbi, Mwatuangi, Asa
Kenya	Boran	Waqa
Kenya	Digo	Mulungu
Kenya	Duruma	Mulungu
Kenya	Elgeyo	Asis
Kenya	Embu	Ngai
Kenya	Gikuyu	Murungu, Ngai, Mwenenyaga
Kenya	Giryama	Mulungu
Kenya	Gush	Erioba (Sun)
Kenya	Kamasya	Asis
Kenya	Kipsgis	Asis, Chebtalel, Cheptalel, Chebango, Ngolo
Kenya	Kony	Asis
Kenya	Maasai	En-kai, Engai, N'gai, Ai, Parsai, Emayian
Kenya	Meru	Murungu, Ngai, Mwene inya
Kenya	Nandi	Asis, Cheptalil Chepkeliensokol or Chepkelienpokol, Chepokoiyo, Chebonamuni
Kenya	Okiet	Asis
Kenya	Oromo	Waqa
Kenya	Pokomo	Muungu
Kenya	Pokot	Tororut, Ilat
Kenya	Rabai	Mulungu
Kenya	Teita	Mlungu
Kenya	Turkana	Akuj
Kenya	Vugusu	Wele
Kenya	Luo	Nyasaye, Wang' Chieng', Nyakolaga, Were, Tham, Wuonwa, Wuon kwere, Wuon ji, Ja Mrima, Jan'gwono, Jahera, Nyakalaga, Janen, Wuon Ogendni, Hono, Polo, Wuon lowo,

		Ratego, Jalweny, Kwar ji, Rahuma, Piny k'nyal, Wuon oru, Ruodh Ruodhi, Wang' Chieng', Nyakolaga, Uworo
Lesotho	**Basut**	Molimo
Lesotho	**Sotho**	Molimo, Molimo o matle
Liberia	**Kissi**	Hala
Liberia	**Kpelle**	Yala
Liberia	**Vai**	Kamba
Malawi	**Tumbuka**	Chiuta, Mulengi, Leza, Mwati, Mweni-Nkongono, Kajilengi, Wamtatakuya, Cinyetenyete, Mweneco, Mupi, Cilera-balanda, Karonga wa mabanja, Cimbatakwinya, Kamphanda, Kamanyimanyi, Wamalumya
Malawi	**Matengo**	Ciuta, Mulungu, Mlezi, Cisumphi
Malawi	**Ngonde**	Kyala, Mbepo Mwikemo, Mdolombwike, Kamanyimanyi, Mpoki
Malawi	**Ngoni**	Unkurukuru, Utixo, Inkosi, Umkulunqango, Uluhlanga, Umkulu, Kakulu, Umnikaze we zinto zonke
Malawi	**Nyanja**	Mulungu, Cuata, Leza, Mphamba, Cisumphi, Cimjili Namalenga or Nyamalenga or Mlengi
Malawi	**Yao**	Mulungu
Malawi	**Tonga**	Tilo, Chiuta or Ciuta, Leza, Mlengi, Chata, Nyangoi, Wamuyaya, Wanthazizose, Mkana Nyifwa, Kajeti, Mtaski, Msungi, Mlezi, Mlengavuwa, Mnanda, Mananda, Mangazi
Malawi	**Chewa**	Mulungu, Namalenga, Leza,

Chapter seven Ezenweke, Elizabeth Onyedinma, in
Ezenweke, Elizabeth Onyedinma (Ed.)
Whose God Is God? Exploring The Concept Of God Within Religions
London & Abuja, Adonis & Abbey Pulishers

		Cham'njili, Mphambe, Chisumphi, Chanta, Mlengi, Mlamulili, Mcizi, Mpulumutsi, Mlezi, Wolera, Mtetezi, Muweluzi
Mali	Mambara	Jalang
Mali	Mdinge	Gala, Guele, Jalang
Mozambiue	Chopi	Tilo
Mozambiue	Yao	Mulungu
	Thongs	Tilo, Hosi, Xikwembu
Namibia	Herero	Nguluvi
Namibia	Kung	Khu, Xu, Xuba, Huwa
Namibia	Nama	Tsui-Goeb, (Supreme Being), Cagn or Kaang, Khub, Nanub
Namibia	San	Urezhwa
Nigeria	Afusare	Daxunum
Nigeria	Basa	Agwatana
Nigeria	Pyem	Wudidi
Nigeria	Rishuwa	Kashiri, Kasiri
Nigeria	Rukuba	Katakuru
Nigeria	Rumaiya	Kashillo, Kashira
Nigeria	Srubu	Kasiri, Kahiri
Nigeria	Binawa	Kashiri
Nigeria	Chawai	Bawai
Nigeria	Dorei	Nillah
Nigeria	Dungi	Kasiri, Kashira
Nigeria	Edo	Osanobua, Osa
Nigeria	Egede	Ohe
Nigeria	Gbari Ibibio	Shekohi, Sheshu, Soko, Esse, Sheko Abassi, Chuku
Nigeria	Idoma	Owo, Owoico
Nigeria	Igbira	Hinegba, Ihinegba
Nigeria	Igbo	Chukwu, Chi, Chineke, Olisa bi n'igwé

Chapter seven Ezenweke, Elizabeth Onyedinma, in
Ezenweke, Elizabeth Onyedinma (Ed.)
Whose God Is God? Exploring The Concept Of God Within Religions
London & Abuja, Adonis & Abbey Pulishers

Nigeria	Ijaw	Egbesu
Nigeria	Indem	Osowo
Nigeria	Itsekiri	Oritse
Nigeria	Iyala	Owo
Nigeria	Jukun	Shido or Chido, Ama or Ma Kadara Onum
Nigeria	Kadara	Onum
Nigeria	Kangoro	Gwaza
Nigeria	Kaibi	Kashiri or Kashira
Nigeria	Katab	Gwaza
Nigeria	Kitmi	Kashila or Kashiri
Nigeria	Kurama	Ashili, Bakashili
Nigeria	Nkum	Oshowo, Ebutokpabi
Nigeria	Nupe	Soko
Nigeria	Orri	Lokpata
Nigeria	Piti	Ure
Nigeria	Songhay	Yerkoy
Nigeria	Tiv	Aondo
Nigeria	UrhoboIsoko	Oghene, Oghenukpabe
Nigeria	Yachi	Phahia
Nigeria	Yako	Ubasi
Nigeria	Yoruba	Olodumare, Olorun, Olofin-Orun
Rwanda	Banyarwanda	Imana, Hategekimana, Hashakimana, Habyarimana, Ndagijimana, Habimana, Bizimana, Bigirimana, Ruremakwaci
Senegal	Serer	Rog
Sierra Leone	Kono	Meketa, Yataa
Sierra Leone	Limba	Kanu, Masala, Masaranka
Sierra Leone	Mendi	Ngewo, Leve

Chapter seven | Ezenweke, Elizabeth Onyedinma, in
Ezenweke, Elizabeth Onyedinma (Ed.)
Whose God Is God? Exploring The Concept Of God Within Religions
London & Abuja, Adonis & Abbey Pulishers

Sierra Leone	Shebro- Bullom- Krim	Hobatoke
Sierra Leone	Temne	Kuru, Kurumasaba
South Africa	Bavenda	Raluvhimba, Mwari
South Africa	Fingo	Qamata
South Africa	Hottentos	Utixo
South Africa	Luvedu	Khuzwane, Mwari
South Africa	Pondo	uDali, uMenzi, u Tixo
South Africa	Tembu	uTixo
South Africa	Thongs	Tilo, Hosi, Xikwembu
South Africa	Tlhaping	Modimo
South Africa	Tswana	Modimo
South Africa	Venda	Nwali
South Africa	Xam	Kaang, Kaggen, Huwu or Huwe
South Africa	Xhosa	U Thixo, uDali, (Maker, Creator), uMenzi, uHlanga, Qamata
South Africa	Zulu	Unkulunkulu, Inkosi, uDumakade, uGobungqongqo, uGuqabadele, uKqili, uMabonga-kutuk-izizwe-zonke, uSomoganiso, uZivelele.
Sudan	Anuak	Juok

Chapter seven — Ezenweke, Elizabeth Onyedinma, in Ezenweke, Elizabeth Onyedinma (Ed.) *Whose God Is God? Exploring The Concept Of God Within Religions* London & Abuja, Adonis & Abbey Pulishers

Sudan	Azande	Mbori or Mboli, Bapaizegino
Sudan	Bari	Ngun
Sudan	Beir	Tummu
Sudan	Bongo	Loma, Hege
Sudan	Didinga	Tamukujen
Sudan	Dilling	Abradi
Sudan	Dinka	Nhialic, Acek, Jok
Sudan	Fajulu	Ngun
Sudan	Gaalin	Allat, Uzza, Manat
Sudan	Jumjum	Dyong
Sudan	Mondari-Ngun	Ngun
Sudan	Kuku	Uletet, Ngulaitait or Nguletet
Sudan	Lokoiya	Oicok
Sudan	Lotuko	Ajok, Naijok
Sudan	Mahraka	Mboli
Sudan	Meban	Juong
Sudan	Moru	Lu
Sudan	Ndogo	Mbiri, Mviri
Sudan	Nuba	Kalo, Elo, Bel, Bel Epti, Kando, Kwarak, Masala, Elem
Sudan	Nuer	Kwoth
Sudan	Shilluk	Juok
Sudan	Toposa	Nakwuge
Swaziland	Swazi	Mkulumncandi, Umkhulumncandi, Inkosatana, Umvelingquangi
Tanzania	Arusha	Engai
Tanzania	Luguru	Mulungu
Tanzania	Maasai	En-kai, Engai, N'gai, Ai, Parsai, Emayian
Tanzania	Nyakyusa	Kyala, Tenende, Nkurumuke, Chata Kyaubiri, Kalesi, Ndorombwike, Mperi
Tanzania	Pare	Kyumbi, Mrungu, Izuva

Chapter seven	Ezenweke, Elizabeth Onyedinma, in Ezenweke, Elizabeth Onyedinma (Ed.) *Whose God Is God? Exploring The Concept Of God Within Religions* London & Abuja, Adonis & Abbey Pulishers

Tanzania	Safwa	Nguruvi
Tanzania	Sandawe	Waronge, Murungu
Tanzania	Sonjo	Mugwe, Riob
Tanzania	Turu	Murungu, Matunda
Tanzania	Zinza	Isewahanga, Kazoba, Rugaba
Tanzania		
Tanzania		
Tanzania		
Tanzania	Bena	Mulungu
Tanzania	Bondei	Mlungu
Tanzania	Chagga	Ruwa
Togo	Ewe	Mawu
Togo	Krachi	Wulbari
Uganda	Acholi	Juok or Jok, Lubanga
	Alur	Jok, Jok Rubanga, Jok Nyakaswiya, Jok Odudu, Jok Adranga, Jok Atar
Uganda	Amba	Nyakara
Uganda	Ankore	Ruhanga, Nyamuhanga, Omuhangi, Rugaba, Kazooba, Mukameiguru, Kazooba Nyamuhanga
Uganda	Bakene	Gasani
Uganda	Banyoro	Ruhanga.
Uganda	Basoga	Kibumba, Kiduma, Kyaka, Nambubi, Lubanga
Uganda	Ganda	Katonda, Kagingo, Mukama, Ssewannaku, Ddunda, Lugaba, Ssebintu, Liisoddene, Nnyiniggulu, Kazooba, Namuginga, Ssewaunaku, Gguluddene, Namugereka
Uganda	Gisu	Wele or Weri, Omubumbi, Wele Wehangagi

Uganda	Gwere	Kibumba
Uganda	Jie	Akuj
Uganda	Karamoja	Akuj
Uganda	Kiga	Ruhanga, Sebahanga, Kazoba, Rugaba, Biheko
Uganda	Kyiga	Weri
Uganda	Lango	Jok
Uganda	Lugbara	Adroa or Adronga, Adro
Uganda	Madi	Ori, Rabanga
Uganda	SEBEI	Oiki, Oinotet
Uganda	Teso	Akuj, Apap, Edeke, Lokasuban
Uganda	Teuso	Didikwari, Nakwit
Zambia	Ambo	Lesa, Cuta
Zambia	Aushi	Makumba
Zambia	Barotse	Lesa, Nyambe
Zambia	Bemba	Lesa, Mulungu, Mwandanshi, Tengenene, Katebebe, Kaleka-Misuma, Kapekape, Kalamfya-Milalo, Kanshiwabikwa, Kashawaliko, Mulopwe, Mwinetwalo, Nalusandulula, Naluntuntwe, Nalwebela, Nafukatila, Kalenga, Nakabumba, Ndubulwila
Zambia	Lala	Lesa, Mulenga, Cuuta, Lucele
Zambia	Kaonde	Lesa
Zambia	Lamba	Lesa
Zambia	Lozi	Nyambe
Zambia	Luapula	Lesa
Zambia	Nyanja	Mulungu, Cuata, Leza, Mphamba, Cisumphi, Cimjili Namalenga or Nyamalenga or Mlengi
Zambia	Ila	Leza, Chilenga, Lubumba, Shakapanga, Namulenga,

Chapter seven Ezenweke, Elizabeth Onyedinma, in
Ezenweke, Elizabeth Onyedinma (Ed.)
Whose God Is God? Exploring The Concept Of God Within Religions
London & Abuja, Adonis & Abbey Pulishers

		Mutalabala, Namakungwe, Muninde, Chaba, Ipaokubozha, Ushatwakwe, Shakatabwa, Mangwe, Shakemba, Kemba, Namesi, Munamazuba, Luvhunabaumba, Mukubwe, Chembwe, Munakasungwe, Chaba-wakaaba-ochitadiwa, Shikakunamo
Zambia	Tonga	Tilo, Chiuta or Ciuta, Leza, Mlengi, Chata, Nyangoi, Wamu yaya, Wanthazizose, Mkana Nyifwa, Kajeti, Mtaski, Msungi, Mlezi, Mlengavuwa, Mnanda, Mananda, Mangazi
Zimbabwe	Shona	Mwari, Nyadenga, Wokumusoro, Gore, Runji, Chipindikure, Chirozva-mauya Chirazamauya, Sagomakoma, Musiki, Muvumbi, Marure, Musikavanhu, Dzivaguru, Chidziva, Mutangakugara, Muwanikwa, Mupavose, Wemumbepo, Muponesi, Muyaradzi, Muratidzi
Zimbabwe	Karanga	Nyadenga
Zimbabwe	Korekore	Wokumusoro, Musiki, Chikara, Dzivaguru
Zimbabwe	Ndebele	Unkulunkulu, Umlimo, Mwali

Myths of Origin

There are various shades of views on the origin of the awareness of God even among renowned scholars. Ekeke and Ekeopkara (2010) corroborate that the three relatively popular views on this matter are through; reflection on the universe, observation of the forces of nature and through the realization of the limitations of man.

It is also believed that it is by reflecting on the wonders of the universe, the sky, the roaring thunders and the stretching of the sky and the wondrous nature of the whole universe. Through the reflections on the universe, therefore, their imagination led them to conclude that there must be a Supersensible Being whose powers not only created this vast and complex universe but also sustains it. Africans unavoidably, came to the realization of the existence of God and its eminent belief in God the creator and sustainer of the universe.

Secondly, closely related to the realization of the universe is the observation of the continual movement and interaction of the forces of the universe. Africans observed that the forces of the universe maintain a constant equilibrium. They observed the day and night as the night constantly breaks into day and the day turns into night. They observed the changes of the weather all year round; they observed the roaring sea waters, the storms, thunder and lightening, and other universal phenomena. They observed the endless firmament, and all the heavenly beings such as the sun, moon and stars, seeing their enormous benefit to man yet unreachable. Ekeke and Ekeokpara conclude that:

> The Africans began to associate the sky with a great God, who is very close to man, supplying man's needs such as rain for his land to produce abundant fruit. From time immemorial; man has been in the habit of looking at the forces of nature with awe and reverence. This made man to worship these forces as having one supernatural power or another. (p.111)

Thirdly, it is further believed that Africans realized the weakness of man, the feeble, insatiable characteristics of all that is created and appreciated, their weakness in all respects; knowledge, power, character and in learning and needed a dependable force and found this on this mighty God, hence they believed in God. Through this realization of man's limitations, Africans realized the existence of God. Ekeke and Ekeokpara (2010) have summarized that:

> Africans saw that they were limited and weak in many respects, including knowledge and power, particularly in the face of death, calamity, thunderstorms, earthquakes, mighty rivers and great forests which are beyond man to control. These limitations and powerlessness rather led them to speculate that there must be a Supreme Being who is superior to these other powers that can be drawn to help them through appeasement and or sacrifice. This made Africans to feel that they needed the help of this Supreme Being in their experiences of limitations and powerlessness. This is the Great God that the Africans worship. (pp. 110-111).

One may say, therefore, that the origin of the belief in God has no date but as old as the very first man. However, three assumptions underline the origin of the belief in God by Africans, man's reflection on the universe, his observation of the forces of nature and his realization of the limitations and weakness of man.

God in African Perspective: Concepts

As in many other world religions, Africans believe in the existence of one God. This is common to the three Abrahamic religions. For instance, in Judaism, there is no God apart from Yahweh and there is no lesser or similar Yahweh. Likewise, in Islam, there is no god but God (Allah). It is an apostasy to compare Allah with any other god.

The above situation clearly demonstrates the concept of God in Africa. In any African language, God has a name as earlier documented in this work and there is no question of qualifying that name to apply to another being. It is unthinkable for the Igbo people of eastern Nigeria to have another or lesser Chineke, the Yoruba of western Nigeria to have more than one Olodumare or Olorun, for Sonata of Congo to have another Nja, for Konso of Ethiopia to have another Bamballe and for Asante of Ghana and Côte d'Ivoire to have another Nyam.

Thus, the Supreme Being in Africa has the highest status in the hierarchy of beings. He is the Creator of all that is created and has the whole world in his palm. He designed the earth and all therein and named all that exists. He is known and described my various attributes. Thus, the uniqueness of God in African perspective cannot be over estimated. The idea of referring to some creatures as lesser gods or minor gods is not acceptable in African traditional religion. The observed anomaly is often witnessed due to linguistic problems arising from the so-called modern languages like English and its impotency of proper translation of certain traditional words

God in African Perspective: Attributes

The concept of God refers to what God is to Africans while His attributes refer to what God actually does for the people rather than what God is. The names given to the Supreme Being of Africans are not shared by any other creatures but are sole prerogatives of the Supreme Being, so are his attributes. Though modernization and globalization have filtered into the very fabrics of the lives of Africans with its effect on their philosophies, it is so on attributing God's attributes to other creatures.

It is important to note that potentials or traits of the Supreme Being in African ontology are anthropomorphic in nature. Ekeke and Ekeopara (2010) affirmed that "Any religion that stripes the Supreme Being of anthropomorphic phenomenon will eventually end up as an abstract religion that does not have human feelings and is not fully realizable in the world.p.211. The use of anthropomorphism terms for God is a universal issue; it is not unique to African Traditional religion. This is so because; God is an abstract term that cannot be comprehended by the human mind. Man, therefore, needs what is seen and known to understand what is not seen and known. Some of these attributes include:

The Creator

In the pyramid of beings, Africans unianimously recognize the Supreme Being as the sole Being at the apex of all beings. They demonstrate the existence of the Supreme Being through a variety and multiplicity of names, songs, arts and evryday life issues. One of the most astounding attributes of the Supreme Being is the originator of all that exists.

It is widely believed in Africa that God, the Supreme Being, created all the created beings both in the heaven, on earth and in the underworld. This is evident in the many names God is known in Africa for. For instance, the Igbo people of eastern Nigeria call him *Chineke* from *Chi Na eke* where Chi = God, Na = that and eke = creates. Same and similar phrases are found in various cultures in Africa. Thus, Osanobwa among the Edo, Eledaa among the Yoruba, Aondo among the Tiv and Soko among the Nupe, all from Nigeria refer to God as the creator. The Igbo of Nigeria also call God *mmanite na ogwugwu ihe niine* connoting Source Being which connotes the Beginning, end and Originator of all beings while *Osanobua* or *Osanobwa* among the Edo of Nigeria, as noted above, connotes the Originator or source of all beings who in addition, carries and sustains the world or universe.

Transcendent and Immanent

The transcendence and immanence attributes of God are two words that may seem contradictory to some people with insufficient knowledge of God but, in actual fact, they are complementary. One would wonder how God may be far removed from his creatures and at the same time very close to them. Yes, God is removed from the daily activities of man, and yet, lives within them since he is a spirit. The transcendence of God is demonstrated in various African myths. For instance, the Igbo people of Nigeria, the Akan of Ghana and Côte d'Ivoire and many other African tribes share the same view that the Supreme Being once lived among men and was interacting with them on day to day busssiness but that after being continually struck by the pestle of an old woman pounding fufu, a traditional food, he moved into the sky. (Jones, 2005) But many other tribes, Igbo people in particular, hold that God was disturbed by women who cook late super and use to hit and disturb him with their pestle when he retired for the day.As a result, he moved farer away above the sky where pestles can no longer reach. Thus, the Igbo people and Yoruba people of Nigeria call him *Chi bi n'igwe* (God who lives in the sky) and *Oba Orun* (King above or heavenly king) respectively. This resonates well with the view of the Mende people of Sierra-Leone that calls God *Ngewo*, meaning the eternal one who rules from above. (Awolalu and Dopamu, 1975).

However, the transcendence nature of God does not undermine his immanence. This is aptly shown by *Chi bi n'igwe ma ogodo ya n'akpu na ana* (God lives in the sky but his cloth is touching the ground) among the Igbo people. This goes on to demonstrate the mighty attributes of God, that even though he lives above the sky, his garments touches the ground, thus making him still among his creatures.

Omnipresence

Closely related to the immanence attribute of God is his omnipresence nature. African people believe that God is everywhere and at the same time. He sees everything everywhere at the same time. This is potrayed in many traditional names and songs.

Omnipotent

God in African ontology is omnipotent, meaning that He is almighty, immense, and massive and all-powerful. All powers in heaven, on earth and in the underworld belong to him and to him alone. Ugwu and Ugwueye (2004) affirm that:

> The concept of God's omnipotence is emphasized in the Nupe song: God is in the front, He is in the back. The Edo name for God "Osanobwa" implies God who carries and sustains the universe. This shows that God is the powerful one, the source of power for all things visible and invisible. The Yoruba say that God is one "who sees both the inside and outside of man". P.35

Many Igbo names also demonstrate the omnipotence and supremacy of God. Such names include:

a. Chinwike – God has all the powers.
b. Chijike – God holds all powers.

c. Chikasi – God is most supreme.
   d. Ifeanyichukwu – Nothing surpasses God.
   e. Chukwuebuka – God is mighty.

Omniscience

This gives the notion of God knowing everything. Nothing is hidden from him. He sees clearly even in the dark. This notion of God has a lot of moral and security implication. It polices the activities of the believers that one does not need to be monitored for one to know that God is casting his eyes on him. The Igbo people normally refer to God as *Anya-na-ene-uwa* (The eye that sees the world). God is the knower of all things and also the compendium of all that should be known. They further reflect these attributes in their names, songs and arts. Such names include:

   a. Chima – God knows
   b. Chimuchem – God knows my thought
   c. Chimazulu – God knows everything
   d. Chihurum – God sees everything

Jugde

God is conceived as the impartial judge. He judges, vindicates and punishes accordingly. Though he is very merciful, he is also a just God at the same time. Thus, the Igbo call him Onye ikpe (judge) and bear names as:

   a. Chinwokwu
   b. Chijiokwu
   c. Chinwikpe

Infinite, Immortal and Imperishable

In Africa, God is not known as one who will one day vanish or die. No, he lives for ever and has no beginning or end. He is eternal and immortal. He is the Ever-living Reality, Ever-living water, and rock of ages, immovable rock and many of such names. The idea of rock is to portray durability and eternity. The Kono people of Sierra Leone also call God *Meketa* meaning "the Everlasting One", "The One who remains and does not die"

In summarizing the attributes of God in African ontology, Brown (1975) succinctly averred that:

> He is the power and the kingdom and the glory and the majesty and to Him belongs creation and the rule over what He created: He alone is the Giver of life; He is omniscient, for His knowledge encompasseth all things, from the deepest depths of the earth to the highest heights of the heavens. The smallest atom in the earth or the heavens is known unto Him. He is aware of how the ants creep upon the hard rock in the darkness of the night. He perceives the movement of specks of dust in the air. He beholds the thoughts which pass through the minds of men, and the range of their fancies and thesecrets of their hearts, by His knowledge, which was from aforetime (p. 2).

Africans have tried to potray God in so many ways depending on how best they think God can be described. God is everything good to them. God is the 'Leaf' that covers the whole world, the 'Fountain of water' that never dries up, the 'Source of full satisfaction' and so on. (Ekeke and Ekeokpara, 1975).

Surbodinates of God in African Theocracy

The belief in a group of beings known as divinities is widely held in African Traditional religions. They are known by various names at various communities. They are seen as surbodinates to the Supreme being and intermediaries between man and God.

They are also commonly referred to as gods, demigods, nature gods/spirits and/or divinities. In his book – Concept of God in Africa, Mbiti explains that the term divinities demonstrates the personification of God's activities and manifestations, nature spirits, deified heroes, and mythological figures.

Scholars have documented that in Yoruba land alone, there are as many as 600 to 1700 divinities (Idowu, 1975). In Edo of Nigeria, Mbiti further narrates that there are as many divinities as there are human needs. He avers that "one [divinity] is connected with wealth, human fertility, and supply of children (*Oluku*); another is iron (*Ogu*), another of medicine (*Osu*), and another of death (*Ogiuwu*)" p.119

In Igbo land too, there are various divinities for various purposes similar to the case of Yoruba shown above. However, the prominent ones are ala/ana/ani (earth divinity), Amadioha (god of justice in form of thunder), Ihejioku, Ogwugwu, Udo and many others. Similar divinities are found in many other west African states.

Reference

Awolalu, J. O. & Dopamu, P. A. (1979). *West African Traditional Religion*. Ibadan: Onibonoje.

Brown, D. A. (1975). *A Guide to Religions*. London: SPCK.

Ekeke, E. C. & Ekeokpara, C. A. (2010). God, Divinities and Spirits in African Traditional Religious Ontology in American Journal of Social and Management Sciences. http://www.scihub.org/AJSMS.

Idowu, E. B. (1973). *African Traditional Religion: A Definition*. London: SCM.

Idowu, B. (1977). *Olodumare: God in Yoruba Belief*. London: Longman.

Karade, B. (1994). *The Handbook of Yoruba Religious Concepts*. York Beach, MA: Samuel Weiser Inc.

Mbiti, J. S. (1969). *Introduction to African Religions*. London: Sheldon.

Mbiti, J. S. (1970). *Concepts of God in Africa*. Nairobi: SPCK.

Parrinder, G. (1977). *West African Traditional Religion*. London: Epworth.

Ugwu, C. O. T. & Ugwueye, L. K. (2004). *African Traditional Religion: A prolegomenon*. Lagos: Merit.

CHAPTER EIGHT

Chi N'eye Ndu: God in an Igbo-African Category

Kanu, Ikechukwu Anthony (OSA)

Introduction

At the time when ideological race struggle was at its peak, Gobineau (1915) developed a biased anthropology, which placed human beings on a hierarchy with Africa at the bottom. He argued that Europe had attained civilization while others are yet to. Following the same line of thought, Hume (cited by Chukwudi 1998) wrote, "I am apt to suspect that the Negroes are to be naturally inferior to the whites. There scarcely ever was a civilized nation of that complexion or even an individual eminent in action or speculation" (p. 214). Hegel (1956), following the same derogatory path wrote further about the negro:

> In Negro life the characteristic point is the fact that consciousness had not yet attained to the realisation of any substantial existence.... Thus distinction between himself as an individual and the universality of his essential being, the African in the uniform, undeveloped oneness of his existence has not yet attained. (p. 93).

He, thus, posits that the Negro is yet to go beyond his instinctual behaviour to identify a being outside of himself. Following the same line of thought, Levy-Bruhl (cited by Njoku 1993), questioned the veracity of an untutored African knowing about God. Corroborating with Levy-Bruhl, Baker (cited in Richard 1964) wrote:

> The Negro is still at the rude dawn of faith-fetishism and has barely advanced in idolatry.... he has never grasped the idea of a personal deity, a duty in life, a moral code, or a shame of lying. He rarely believes in a future state of reward and punishment, which whether true or not are infallible indices of human progress". (p. 199).

Chi n'eye ndu as an understanding of God in Igbo-African category is a thesis that has far gone beyond proving that the African

can know or concieve God. It has moved from the wider parameters of theology to the particular aperture of Christological investigation. It investigates the possibility of an understanding of the Christ-God within an African category. The idea employed here is that of an Igbo-African. This concept is very significant because the Igbo race shared in the African worldview, and the interactive nature of the African worldview, makes this consideration more relevant. This Christological perspectives constructed from the Igbo worldview creates a socio-political context, which agrees with the perspective of Schreiter (1985), who maintains that theology is meant for a community and not to remain the property of a theologian class. It is not an elitist enterprise. It begins from below, from the underside of history, its main interlocutors, the poor and the culturally marginalized. It responds to the question: "how will Christ and his message be presented to the Igbo person, in such a way that he or she would understand and appreciate Jesus within categories that he or she is at home with?" This piece adds to the ongoing developments in Christology during the past thirty three years as evident in the works of Nyamity (1984), Sanon (1991), Kabasele (1991), Kolie (1991), Magessa (1991), Walligo (1991), Waruta (1991), Bujo (1992), Ukachukwu (1992) among other scholars who have searched for an authentic African response to the Christ event.

From Biblical and Patristic Christology to an Igbo Christology

The followers of Jesus acknowledged him as the Messiah (Christos, the anointed one), the expected anointed King of David's royal line; whether in the combination of Jesus Christ or Christ, it quickly became equivalent to a personal name. The Aramaic Hebrew speaking Christians, closest to the life, death and resurrection of Jesus, understood him as "the Son of Man", "the Messiah", "Son of David" and "Son of God". The Jewish Greek converts to Christianity translated Christ as Christos, and they understood him as the centre of the cosmos or universe. For the Hellenistic Gentile Christians, Christ is the Eternal Divine Logos and the Wisdom of God.

Chapter eight	Kanu, Ikechukwu Anthony (Osa), in Ezenweke, Elizabeth Onyedinma (Ed.) *Whose God Is God? Exploring The Concept Of God Within Religions* London & Abuja, Adonis & Abbey Pulishers

According to Kankai (2008), the different authors of the gospels presented Christologies that responded to particular situations and cultures. Mark the evangelist presented Jesus as healer and exorcist. In the first chapter, he narrates that Jesus cast out demons and healed the mother-in-law of Simon. As a consequence, people were immediately drawn to him with confidence because of his power to heal. In addition to highlighting Jesus as healer and exorcist, Jesus is designated as a faithful and suffering servant of God. In Matthew's gospel, he is the Son of David, King of Nations, the New Moses and the Lawgiver. The Evangelist Luke presented a Jesus who is a prophet and advocate of the poor, and a person of prayer. In John's gospel, he is the Pre-existent Word, Eternal Wisdom, Revelation of God's Glory and the One Who Is.

During the Patristic period, the Christology of the Fathers was profoundly biblical. For them, Christ is the ultimate meaning of all scripture. They believed that every text of the bible reflects and expresses a moment or aspect of one plan of salvation or the other, in which the Old Testament prepares and anticipates Christ. During this period, heresies about the nature of Christ also emerged. Docetism proposed that Jesus was not truly human but merely apparent to be man. For the Gnostics, Christ is the spiritual being fully aware of his divine identity, and whose mission is to reveal to his followers the secret of their divine identity. Adoptionism teaches that Jesus was a man whom God adopted to be his son.

The Arians taught that the logos and Jesus were not two beings but one, since the logos has indeed become flesh. Thus, the logos is not God since he cannot be God and man at the same time. Unlike the Arians, the Appollinarians denied the existence of a rational human soul in Christ, because they believed that the logos uniting with Jesus takes the place of a rational soul. During the Council of Ephesus, the Fathers declared that the same Jesus Christ is perfect God and perfect man, composed of a rational soul and body, consubstantial to the Father as to his divinity and consubstantial to us as to his humanity. Thus, Christ has two natures, divine and human. The Council of

Chalcedon further emphasized that Jesus has two natures, without confusion and change, without division and separation (Kanu 2012).

From the above observations, it is obvious that these Christologies emphasize the divinity of Jesus. This is referred to as a high or descending Christology or Christology from above. It emphasizes the exalted and high quality of Jesus. This method of Christologizing goes back to the gospel of St John, which in fact has a high Christology. Low Christology, different from high Christology concentrates on the man Jesus, his humanity. This Christology has opened interesting possibilities, producing a whole new set of categories such as Jesus as the man for others, the revolutionary, the way, the representative and the harlequin. While western Christology could be considered as high, the African approach to Christology is quite different. It begins from below and ascends above (Kanu, 2012).

An Understanding of Nd'igbo of Nigeria

According to Onuh (1991), by way of definition, "Igbo" is both a language and the name of an ethnic group or tribe in Nigeria. There is, however, an etymological and lexical complexity surrounding the meaning of the term 'Igbo'. In the contention of Ekwuru (2009), the difficulty of arriving at a precise etymological and semantic clarity of the word "Igbo" has its trace in the unprecise nature of the history of the Igbo people. For Afigbo (1975a), compared to the state of research as regards origin in relation to other tribes in Nigeria, the Igbo history can without much exaggeration be described as *terra incognita*. However, Afigbo (1975b) further observes that the Igbos are not indifferent to this crisis of identity. Their experience of colonialism, and even the Biafran Civil War has sparked off in them the quest for a historical identity. It is such that Isichei (1976) avers that no historical question arouses more interest among the present day Igbo people than the enquiry "where did the Igbo come from?"

As regards the territorial identity of the Igbos, Uzozie (1991) observes that "To date, there is no agreement among ethnographers, missionaries, anthropologists, historians, geographers and politicians on the definition and geographical limits of territory" (p. 4). Ekwuru

---

Chapter eight | Kanu, Ikechukwu Anthony (Osa), in
Ezenweke, Elizabeth Onyedinma (Ed.)
Whose God Is God? Exploring The Concept Of God Within Religions
London & Abuja, Adonis & Abbey Pulishers

(2009) states that any attempt to introduce who the Igbo is poses a lot of problems in all aspects of its academic conceptualizations. This, notwithstanding, Hatch (1967) describes the Igbo people as a single people even though fragmented and scattered, inhabiting a geographical area stretching from Benin to Igala and Cross River to Niger Delta. They speak the same language which gradually developed various dialects but understood among all the groups. Their cultural patterns are closely related, based on similar cults and social institutions; they believe in a common Supreme Being known as *Chukwu* or *Chineke*. Two theories have emerged in response to the question "where did the Igbo come from?" There is, the Northern Centre Theory which, according to Onwuejeogwu (1987) posits that the Igbos migrated from five northern centre areas, namely: the Semetic Centre of the Near and Far East, the Hermatic Centre around Egypt and Northern Africa, the Western Sahara, the Chadian Centre and the Nok Centre. The second historical hypothesis is the Centre Theory of Igbo Heartland. According to Jones (cited by Isichei 1976), the early migrations of the proto-Igbo originated from the areas termed as the Igbo heartland, such as: Owerri, Okigwe, Orlu and Awka divisions.

Geographically speaking, Njoku (1990) posits that Igboland is located in the Southeastern region of what is known as Nigeria. The Southern part of Nigeria exhibits a wide variety of topographical features. The average temperature is about 85, with annual rainfall of 70 inches. It is situated within the parallels of 6 and 8 east longitudes and 5 and 7 north latitudes. As a culture area, it is made up of Enugu, Anambra, Imo, Abia and parts of the Delta, Cross River, Akwa Ibom and Rivers State of Nigeria. According to Uchendu (1965), in its status as an ethnic group, the Igbo share common boundaries with other ethnic groups: Eastward, the Yakos and Ibibios; westwards, with the Binis and the Isokos, Warri; Northward, with the Igalas, Idomas, and the Tivs, and on the Southward, the Ijaws and Ogonis. Socio-politically, unlike the other tribes in Nigeria, who evolved a molithic centralized system of government, the Igbo distinguish themselves with a complicated socio-political structure which has been qualified

---

Chapter eight | Kanu, Ikechukwu Anthony (Osa), in
Ezenweke, Elizabeth Onyedinma (Ed.)
Whose God Is God? Exploring The Concept Of God Within Religions
London & Abuja, Adonis & Abbey Pulishers

as republican. The Igbo ethnic group is divided into clans, each clan is made up of towns; and each town villages. The village is the primary social unit constituted of families or kindred. The family is the nucleus of society. Politically, the lineage system is the matrix of the social units or organization and provides grounds for political and religious structures (Kanu, 2012). The traditional concepts of political power and authority is structured and determined by their concepts of *umunna* and the membership of the association based on elaborate title system. Economically, Aligwekwe (1991) avers that the traditional Igbo people were sedentary agriculturists. This delimitation of Igboland as a culture area, helps to identify the cultural horizon for the study on the Igbo-African concept of life.

Life in Igbo-African Ontology

The concept of life has been analysed by scholars of various academic disciplines and at different periods. However, the researcher is primarily concerned with the concept of life *ndu* in Igbo anthropology. Igbo traditional thought, like those of other African groups, has perhaps been rightly dubbed heavily anthropocentric and their concept of life and person derives from this perspective (Nwala, 1998). The concept of life in Igbo anthropology can be seen from various perspectives; however, generally, it is a road-map that reveals the Igbo conceptual and historical construct of life possibilities and human potentialities, with built-in goals and values for communal and individual self-determination. For a better appreciation of the Igbo concept of life, there is need to explore the historical-cultural roots of the Igbo.

Life as the Highest Good

The desire for life *ndu* and its preservation in Igbo ontology is the *summum bonum* (the supreme good), and every other thing is expected to serve its realization (Nwala, 1998). The prominent appearance of *ndu* in Igbo proverbs, parables and personal names

---

Chapter eight	Kanu, Ikechukwu Anthony (Osa), in Ezenweke, Elizabeth Onyedinma (Ed.) *Whose God Is God? Exploring The Concept Of God Within Religions* London & Abuja, Adonis & Abbey Pulishers

projects the height of the value the Igbo race places on life. For instance, the Igbo would say,

Ndubisi: life is the first. From this perspective, life is the prime necessity. Life should be pursued before and above every other thing or value.

Ndukaku: life is greater than wealth. This is a little bit related to the first. If life is greater than wealth, then, wealth must not be pursued at the expense of life.

Ndubuizu: life is ethos of consensus. That people are able to come together and discuss and even agree on something is because they have life.

Ndulue: If life stretches out. The plans about the future in the present can only be actualized if life extends into the future.

Ndukwe: If life agrees. This is related to the preceding. The actualization of future plans depends on if life agrees that we be in that future.

Nduka: Life is greater.

Nduamaka: Life is good.

Because of the prime place that life occupies in Igbo philosophy, everything that the Igbo does is geared towards the preservation of life. Eating, drinking, sacrifices, rituals and rites, kinship, taboos and other moral provisions, worship and even the existence of sacred specialists is for the preservation of life. Nothing is done without a bearing to life (Obi, 2009).

Life as Active and Dynamic

Life for the Igbo is not just to exist and be counted as existing at census. It is an active and dynamic existence in which other things follow. Life is the principle of activity, growth and fulfilment. As such, the more elevated there is life, the more effective and efficient will the functions of acting, growth and reproduction. This implies that the value of life is linked with the quality of life. The higher the quality the better the performance; it is a vital force that keeps a person not only in motion, but also in constructive actions that help a person and others live on and better (Obi, 2009). From the above perspective, to say to a man who lives *iwuola* (you are dead), means that the person in question has become inactive or incapacitated in respect to certain functions expected of him as a human being (Nwala, 1998). For instance, the inability of a man to climb a palm tree or to make his wife pregnant can earn a man the expression *iwuola* or *odi ndu onye wuru awu ka mma* (a living that is worse than the dead). If one, however, is able to execute any of the above roles, it earns him or her the expression *idi ndu*.

Life as Given and Sustained by God

A very significant concept of *ndu* among the Igbos is the idea that *ndu* is from God. This makes the human person a theomorphic being. This explains why the Igbos say, *ndu sin a chi* (life is from God). When a child is born it is taken to be a gift from God. The life of children is not attributed to the mere biological fact of conception because every child has existed in an antecedent world of a divine master. It is, thus, not surprising that the Igbo would name their child:

a. **Chi-*nyere ndu:*** God gave life
b. ***Nke-chi-yere:*** The one God has given
c. ***Chi-n'eye ndu:*** God gives life
d. ***Chi-di-ogo:*** God is generous
e. ***Chi-nwe- ndu:*** God owns life
f. ***Chi-ekwe:*** God has agreed
g. ***Chi-ji-ndu:*** God owns life

However, God does not only give a child, he also guides and protects the child all through its existence; this is why the Igbo would say *ndu di n'aka chi* (life is in the hand of God) (Obi, 2009). Even though life is in the hand of God, it is still, for the Igbo, a paradox: meaning that it is unpredictable. It is often interrupted by death. One wonders indefinitely at such enigma, inconsistency, mystery and puzzles of premature death, the absurdity and ambiguity of life and death. It is in this regard that Onunwa echoes that, "Among the unfriendly agents that threaten life here on earth (for the Igbo) is illness. The other enemy which the Igbo hates is death" (Onunwa, 1990, p.81).

Although death is conceived as a transition to the world of the ancestors, it still does not change the fact that it is an enigma. It is, thus, not surprising that the Igbo would name their child: *onwu di njo* (death is bad). *Onwubuche* (death is my worry). *Onwubiko* (death I implore you). *Onwu kam ike* (death is more powerful that I am). *Onwuasoanya* (death is no respecter of persons). *Onwuamaeze* (death does not recognize a king or a great man). In spite of the human person's wisdom and technological know-how, death still defies prediction.

Life as Belongingness

The Igbo world into which a child is born crying *abatala m ya* (I have come into it) is made up of seven characteristics: common origin, common world-view, common language, shared culture, shared race, colour and habits, common historical experience and a common destiny (Pantaleon, 1995). This communal dimension of the African life is expressed in the Igbo proverb, *Ngwere ghara ukwu osisi, aka akpara ya* (If a lizard stays off from the foot of a tree, it would be caught by man). It expresses the indisputable and inevitable presence of, not just the family, but the community to which the individual belongs. The Igbo's believe that "when a man descends from heaven, he descends into a community". The community rejoices and welcomes his arrival, finds out whose reincarnation he is, gives the person a name and interprets that arrival within the circumstance of the birth. As the child grows, he becomes aware of his dependence on his kin group and community (Kanu, 2012). He also realizes the necessity of making his own contribution to the group (Uchendu, 1965). According to Mulago (1989):

> The community is the necessary and sufficient condition for the life of the individual person. The individual person is immersed into the natural world and nevertheless emerges from it as an individual and a person within his conscience and freedom given him by the mediation of the community in which he senses a certain presence of the divine. (p. 115).

During one of the feasts organized by Okonkwo in the work, *Things Fall Apart*, his uncle, Uchendu, expressed the Igbo philosophy of belongingness:

> We do not ask for wealth because he that has health and children will also have wealth. We do not pray to have more money but to have more kinsmen. We are better than animals because we have kinsmen. An animal rubs its itching flank against a tree, a man asks his kinsman to scratch him (Achebe, 2008, p. 132).

After the feast, when one of the eldest men of the *umunna* rose to thank Okonkwo, the reason for the Igbo philosophy of belongingness is revealed with a different shade of insight:

> A man who calls his kinsmen to a feast does not do so to save them from starving. They all have food in their own homes. When we gather together in the moonlit village ground it is not because of the moon. Everyman can see it in his own compound. We come together because it is good for kinsmen to do so (Achebe, 1998, p. 133).

Mbiti has classically proverbialized the community's determining role of the individual life, "I am because we are and since we are, therefore I am" (Mbiti, 1970, p. 108). The community, according to Pantaleon, gives the individual his existence. That existence is not only meaningful, but also possible only in a community (Kanu, 2012). To be is to belong and to belong is to be (Anah, 2005). To be alive is to belong.

The Igbo principle of *Egbe bere Ugo bere* (let the kite perch, let the eagle perch) re-enacts the contents and significance of belongingness as the essence and hermeneatic core of Igbo reality. Pantaleon (1995) believes that what a being is, is its activity of perching (belonging). To perch is to be. To be is to perch. To be is to belong and to belong is to be. Thus, existence for the Igbo is an act of belonging.

Chapter eight | Kanu, Ikechukwu Anthony (Osa), in
Ezenweke, Elizabeth Onyedinma (Ed.)
Whose God Is God? Exploring The Concept Of God Within Religions
London & Abuja, Adonis & Abbey Pulishers

Life as a Circle

Life is circlical for the African. The cyclical nature of life affects the African's concept of time, and also gives a philosophical basis for beliefs such as in reincarnation. The history of the African people, as in that of the Greeks is not a lineal movement. Everything repeats itself. Thus, one moves from day to night, which gives birth to another day, and since man is part of the laws of this world, he moves from life to death and to another life again. This explains why when an African loses time, he does not see it as a loss because he knows another will come.

Life as a Stage

In African ontology, life could be refered to as a play. In a play, according to Jacob (2010), how and when an actor enters the stage is not his or her own making but depends on his or her assigned role in the play. In life, too, where and when a person is born or dies which makes for human superficial differences of race, colour, status etc, is not his own design. Destiny plays a very significant role in the determination of our life. The interference of destiny raises questions as regards freedom and determinism. Moreso, just as an actor may return one or more times to the play stage after once taking an exit in order to complete his or her assigned role, a dead person may also return through reincarnation to the world stage.

Life as Everlastingness

Pantaleon (1995) had argued in his study of the analytic connotations of being as belongingness that to be is to 'be-long', which means, 'to live long'. This is based on the idea that life extends into eternity. Life goes beyond the present dimension of the *Uwa* (World) to the *Uwa* of the ancestors (the world of the ancestors), such that to be and not to be-long is not to be at all. While *on-going* belongingness may be open-ended, *being-long* belongingness stretches into everlastingness. As such, in Pantaleon, one becomes through being-on so as to be-going, in other to be-long, that is to participate in the everlastingness of being.

The Provenance of Human Life in African Ontology

In African ontology, life begins from the conception of the child in the woman. And right from the time the child is conceived, respect is accorded to the child through the rites of passage. In these rites and rituals, the hands of the gods are recognized in the socio-religious community and implored to further effect their authenticity and relevance (Madu, 2011). The rites of passage, as regards the conception of a child, are done to ensure a change of condition from the spiritual world to the physical world. It is celebrated as a new outburst of life following the intervention of the divine. Thus, at the point of conception, it is not just about human involvement, the divine is also involved. This is why, during the rites of pregnancy, the divine order is acknowledged and actualized. In fact, rites of passage are considered to be the re-enactment of the archetypal patterns set by the gods in *illo tempore* (Metuh, 1991).

Very significant is the fact that rites of passage are done for the various stages in the development of the human life and in the life of the traditional people. And every stage is connected to the other and is as significant as the other, for without the early stage, there wouldn't be a later stage.

In the contention of Metuh (1991), "Pregnancy (for the African), is a transitional period between conception and childbirth. And so the ceremonies of pregnancy and childbirth, together, generally constitute one whole" (p. 124). According to Parrinder (1976), "Like some of the seven sacraments, these mark the turning points in life; birth, puberty, marriage and death. They are accompanied with various religious and magical acts" (p. 90).

Pregnancy in African life, is not just about the woman and her choices, it is a community affair. The community bears both the gains and the loses. The *dramatis personae* include: the wife, the husband, neighbours, spirit forces and the unborn baby. The whole pregnancy rite is fashioned to facilitate the birth of the child and to protect the mother and child from evil forces (Madu, 2011).

Among the Igbos of the North Central area of eastern Nigeria, their pregnancy ritual is called *Ima Ogodo*. It involves a series of rites. As soon as conception takes place, there is consultation with the divine about the best way to preserve the pregnancy. The materials used in the rite are symbolic: a dog for sacrifice, a white chalk, ogirishi tree and gravels. When the dog is sacrificed, it is usually a dynamic ceremony for the child, praying that he may be dynamic, visionary, smart and loyal as the dog. The white chalk signifies purity. It is also a symbol of consecration. The ogirishi tree survives under harsh conditions, and has a very long life span. It symbolizes longevity and health. The prayer of the community that brings the origishi tree is that their child may flourish like it. The gravels symbolize permanence, signifying that the child has come to stay. This is the prayer that the priest says during the sacrifice:

> We have planted the ogorishi tree in order that the child born to this woman may flourish like the ogirishi tree. We have set gravels to form the riverbed besides the tree in order for the gravels to remain when the river dries up, so may this woman's child remain alive after the waters of childbirth have broken (Metuh, 1995, p. 125).

In all these, efforts are directed towards protecting the child and securing his future if he is eventually born (Madu, 2011). The various preparations made even before the child is born is based on the African philosophy that life begins even before conception.

Chi in Igbo Ontology

According to Ezewugo (1987), the word *Chi* has three connotations in Igbo ontology: in its narrow and primary sense, it applies to the Supreme Being and carries here the force of a proper name. Secondly, it denotes any being, human or divine that is acting solely in the name and authority of the Supreme Being: *onye kwado ije chi ya akwadobe* (if a person gets ready to go on a journey, his Chi gets ready too); *chi ya edulugoya naba* (His Chi has taken him home with him). Human agents could also be called *Chi* if he or she has acted as an agent of providence to a fellow human being, like saving the life of a person who wants to commit suicide: *chi nwayi bu diya* (a woman's chi is her husband); *ogo bu chi onye* (one's father inlaw is one's chi). *Chi* also has an abstract and impersonal reference to providence. In this case, it refers to a divine decree or fate. The Igbos believe that before a child is born, the course of his life has been charted by his *Chi*: *onye ajo chi kpatalu nku ewa ta ya*.

Chi occupies a significant place in Igbo life and salvation history. It is, therefore, not surprising that many Igbo names have *Chi* attached to it. Like:

a. *Chi azor*: God saves
b. *Chi jioke*: God holds the share
c. *Chi amaka*: God is good
d. *Chi wendu*: God owns life
e. *Oge chi*: God's time
f. *Chi nonye*: God stays with me
g. *Chi merem*: God should do for me
h. *Chi dera*: God has written
i. *Chi naza ekpere:* God answers prayer
j. *Chim dindu*: My God is alive
k. *Chi nedum:* God leads me
l. *Chi azokam*: God saved me
m. *Chi di bere*: God is merciful
n. *Amara chi*: Grace of God
o. *Nke chi yere:* The one given by Chi
p. *Gwa chi:* Tell Chi
q. *Kene chi:* Greet God
r. *Arinze chi*: Were it not for God?
s. *Golibelu chi*: Rejoice unto God

Chi n'eye ndu: God in Igbo Category

A very significant concept of life among the Igbos is the idea that life is from God. This makes the human person a theomorphic being. Thus, the Igbo would say, *ndu sin a chi* (life is from God). When a child is born, it is taken to be a gift from God. The life of children is not attributed to the mere biological fact of conception because every child has existed in an antecedent world of a divine master. It is, thus, not surprising that the Igbo would name their child:

a. *Chi-nyere ndu:* God gave life
b. *Nke-chi-yere:* The one God has given
c. *Chi-n'eye ndu:* God gives life
d. *Chi-di-ogo:* God is generous
e. *Chi-nwe- ndu:* God owns life
f. *Chi-ekwe:* God has agreed
g. *Chi-ji-ndu:* God owns life

However, according to Obioma (2009), God does not only give a child, he also guides and protects the child all through its existence; this is why the Igbo would say *ndu di n'aka chi* (life is in the hand of God).

For the Igbo, life begins from the conception of the child in the woman. And right from the time the child is conceived, respect is accorded to the child through the rites of passage. In these rites and rituals, Madu (2011) states that the hands of the gods are recognized in the socio-religious community and implored to further effect their authenticity and relevance. Thus, Metuh (1991) maintains that the rites of passage, as regards the conception of a child, are done to ensure a change of condition from the spiritual world to the physical world. It is celebrated as a new outburst of life following the intervention of the divine. At the point of conception, it is not just about human involvement, the divine is also involved. This is why, during the rites of pregnancy, the divine order is acknowledged and actualized. In fact, rites of passage are considered to be the re-enactment of the archetypal patterns set by the gods in *illo tempore*.

The concept of the human person in Yoruba ontology further reveals the place of the divine as the source of life. According to Oduwole (2010) Yoruba scholars agree that the human person is made up of three basic elements: *Ara* (body), *Emi* (breath) and *Ori* (soul). Idowu (1962) describes the body as the concrete, tangible thing of flesh and bones which can be known through the senses. As regards the *Emi*, he describes it as spirit, and this is invisible. It is that which gives life to the whole body and thus could be described through its causal functions: its presence in the body of a person determines if the person still lives or is dead. According to Ebunoluwa, the body is the creation of *Orisha nla* (Arch-divinity). He was assigned by *Olodumare* (the Supreme Being) to mould the body of human beings. It is only the Supreme Being that puts the spirit into the body so as to give it life. Yoruba reflections on the human person does not end with the body and spirit. There is a third element called the soul. The soul suggests that the human person already has an individuality in the spiritual world before birth. From this understanding, life does not begin with birth, it rather begins as soon as one acquires the soul which defies a person's individuality. The soul of the human person begins to live even before there is a body for its abode.

From the foregoing, it is generally believed that life comes from God. Thus, the designation of Jesus as the giver of life is not alien to the African but rather makes more sense to him and agrees with what he already believes about God.

Conclusion

This research has investigated the possibility of an understanding of the Christ-God within an African category. The idea employed here is that of an Igbo-African. From the Christological perspective, it responds to the question: "how will Christ and his message be presented to the Igbo person, in such a way that he or she would understand and appreciate Jesus within categories that he or she is at home with?" It is born out of the understanding that Christ's incarnation is not only to be conceived as the in-breaking of the

Chapter eight	Kanu, Ikechukwu Anthony (Osa), in
	Ezenweke, Elizabeth Onyedinma (Ed.)
	Whose God Is God? Exploring The Concept Of God Within Religions
	London & Abuja, Adonis & Abbey Pulishers

divine *Logos* in human history but also as the advent of the mystery of possibilities of his humanization in a variety of cultures. It asserts that God is not a being only expressed in western categories, but can also be received and appreciated within African categories, as in *Chi n'eye ndu:* God who gives life.

References

Achebe, C. (2008). Things Fall Apart. *England.* Heinemann.

Afigbo, E. A. (1975). Towards a History of the Igbo-Speaking People of Nigeria. In F. C. Ogbalu and E. N. Emenanjo (Eds.). *Igbo Language and Culture* (pp. 11-27). Ibadan: Heineman.

Afigbo, E. A. (1975). Prolegomena to the Study of the Culture History of the Igbo-speaking Peoples of Nigeria. In F. C. Ogbalu and E. N. Emenanjo (Eds.). *Language and Culture* (pp. 28-53). Ibadan: Heineman.

Aligwekwe, E. P. (1991). The Continuity of Traditional Values in the African Society: The Igbo of Nigeria: Owerri: Totan.

Bujo, B. (1992). *African Theology in its social Context.* New York: Orbis.

Chukwudi, E. E. (1998). Modern Western Philosophy and Africa Colonialism. In E. E. Chukwudi. *African Philosophy: An Anthology* (pp.200-215). Oxford: Blackwell.

Ekwuru, E. (1999). *The Pangs of African Culture in Traivail.* Owerri: Totan.

Frankfurt: Peterlang.

Gobineau, A. (1915). *The Inequality of Human Race.* London: William Heinemann.

Hegel, G. W. F. (1956). *The Philosophy of History.* New York: Dover.

Idowu, B. (1962). *Olodumare: God in Yoruba Belief.* London: Longman.

Isichei , E. (1976). *A History of the Igbo People.* London: Macmillan.

Kabasele, F. (1991). Christ as Chief. In R. J. Schreiter (Ed.). *Faces of Jesus in Africa*(pp. 103-115). New York: Orbis.

Kankai, P. (2008). Christology. *(Lecture Notes). Jos: St Augustine's Major Seminary, Department of Theology.*

Kanu, I. A. (2012). Towards an African Christology. In E. O. Ezenweke and I. A. Kanu (Eds.). *Issues in African Traditional Religion and Philosophy* (pp. 75-102). Jos: Fab Anieh.

Kanu, I. A. (2012). The Concept of Life and Person in African Anthropology. In E. O. Ezenweke and I. A. Kanu (Eds.). *Issues in African Traditional Religion and Philosophy* (pp. 61-74). Jos: Fab Anieh.

Kanu, I. A. (2012). *The Functionality of Being in Pantaleon's Operative Metaphysics Vis-a-Vis the Niger Delta Conflict.* African Research Review: An International Multi-Disciplinary Journal. 6. 1. 215.

Kanu, I. A. (2012). *Inculturation and the Quest for an Igbo Christology. M.sc Dissertation. Department of Religion and Human Relations, Nnamdi Azikiwe University, Awka.*

Magessa, L. (1991). Christ the Liberator and Africa Today. In R. J. Schreiter *(Ed.).Faces of Jesus in Africa* (pp. 151-163). New York: Orbis.

Madu, J. E. (2011). Rites of Passage in Traditional and Modern Igbo Society.

Metuh, I. E. (1991). African Religions in Western Conceptual Schemes: The Problem of   Interpretation. *Jos: Imico.*

Mulago, V. (1989). *African Heritage and Contemporary Christianity. Nairobi:* Oxford University.

Njoku, F. O. C. (1993). A Phenomenological Critique of the Igbo God-Talk. Encounter: *A Journal of African Life and Religion.* 2. 70-91.

Njoku, E. E. (1990). *The Igbos of Nigeria: Ancient Rites, Changes and Survival.*

New York: Edwin Mellen.

Nwala, T. U. (1998). Igbo Philosophy. *Lagos: Literained.*

Nyamiti, C. (1991). African Christologies Today. In R. J. Schreiter (Ed.). *Faces of Jesus in Africa* (pp. 3-23). New York: Orbis.

Onwuejeogwu, M. A. (1987). Evolutionary Trends in the History of the Development of the Igbo Civilization in the Culture Theatre of Igbo land in Southern Nigeria. A Paper Presented during the Ohiajioku Lecture, Owerri.

Onuh, C. (1991). *Christianity and the Igbo Rites of Passage: The Prospects of Inculturation*. Frankfurt: Peter Lang.

Oduwole, E. (2010). Personhood and Abortion: An African Perspective. In *Personhood and Personal Identity: A Philosophical Study*. Enugu: Snaap.

Onunwa, U. (1990). *Studies in Igbo Traditional Religion*. Obosi: Pacific.

Pantaleon, I. (1995). *Metaphysics: The kpim of Philosophy*. Owerri: IUP.

Parrinder, E. G. (1976). *African Traditional Religion*. London: Sheldon.

Schreiter, R. (1994). *Constructing Local Theologies*. Maryknoll: Orbis.

Sanon, A. (1991). Jesus, Master of Initiation. In R. J. Schreiter (Ed.). *Faces of Jesus in Africa* (pp. 85-102). New York: Orbis.

State. Madu, J. E. (2011). Rites of Passage in Traditional and Modern Igbo Society. *Unpublished Lecture Note. Nnamdi Azikiwe University Awka, Anambra*

State Mbiti, J. S. (1970). African Religions and Philosophy. *Nairobi: East African Educational.*

Ukachukwu, C. M. (1993). *Christ the African king: A New Testament Christology*.

Unpublished Lecture Note. Nnamdi Azikiwe University Awka, Anambra

Uchendu, V. C (1965), *the Igbos of South East Nigeria*. London: Rinehart and Winston.

Waruta, D. W. (1991). Who is Jesus Christ for Africans Today? Priest, Prophet, otentate. In R. J. Schreiter (Ed.). *Faces of Jesus in Africa* (pp. 52-64). New York: Orbis

CHAPTER NINE

God Is God: A Relationship

Ezenweke, Elizabeth Onyedinma

Introduction

As earlier noted in the first chapter of this work, the phenomenon of religion and its practices have been viewed from diverse perspectives and from a wide range of interest and have been shown to be an issue of accord and discord in almost all human societies. It has also been a matter of interest to scholars of religious studies, sociology, anthropology, theology, philosophy, historical studies and lots more. This, coupled with the elusive nature of the subject matter of religion has created multiple and different shades of definitions and concepts of religion and has further made it difficult to have a single generally accepted definition.

However, in any good definition of religion, the relationship between man and the Supreme Being and super- sensible beings must be demonstrated as the core of that definition. Another important element of any good definition is the inclusion of the collection of cultural systems, belief systems, and worldviews that symbolically relate humanity to spirituality.

It is further highlighted in the first chapter of this book that humanity, from its earliest history, has demonstrated dependency on God and other cosmic powers and continually searches for and attempts to maintain a purer relationship with such Beings. However, in an attempt to interract with these Supreme beings that are believed to be invible, there are the existence of various shades of interpretations of this Supreme Being and modes of interracting with them. This has, therefore, resulted in the religion being the major cause of conflicts in many human societies which has hitherto, recorded far reaching consequences on the conduct of social relations and is having manifold implications on sustainable developments in different parts of the world.

Interestingly, from experience as a scholar of Religious Studies and/or a look at comparative religion, one could say without fear of contradiction that people often fight over the same coin with different shades.

The remaining part of this chapter will cast a comparative look at the main essence of some of the known religions with a view to ascertain their similarity and to find enough point to conclude that God is God in all cultures but expresses in various ways as culturally, socially, economically, emotionally and geographically conditioned in those cultures.

Shared Features

It is not arguable that despite doctrinal issues and semantics, virtually all religions share some basic features. Virtually all known major religions have their narratives, symbols, traditions and sacred histories, and often myths of existence. Most of them, if not all, have a hierarchy of leaders and distinct lay faithfuls, have a process of admitting and categorising membership, have a role of classification between leaders and followers, commemoration of historic events in the form of feast, festivals, holidays and abstenance of various forms, belief in divine appointment of leaders and revealation of sacred texts and also inculcate in the adherents how to accommodate anxieties and manage misfortunes by providing sets of answers to how and why things in the world are what and how they are.

Origin Most religions share the same view that their religions were founded on the principle that divine beings or forces can promise a level of justice in a supernatural realm that cannot be perceived in this natural one. (Esptein, 2010) and that the birth of many world religions stemmed from the vision of some charismatic prophet (s) or leader (s) who emerged at various times in history. These charismatic humans or superhumans often convincingly inspired the imaginations of men of their time that were seeking for a more comprehensive answer to their problems than they feel is provided by everyday beliefs. Typical examples to this are the

Muhammed; the founder of Islam and Jesus Christ; the founder of Christianity.

Again, every religion, whether classified as world religion or indigenous religions, or whatever their philosophical origin may be, stemmed from a particular cultural background and so, is ethnic as well. (Fitzgerald, 2000; Prentiss, 2003).

Concept of God

Virtually, if not all religions, believe in the Supreme Being, k nown by many names in various cultures. It is believed that God, Allah or the Supreme Being created every other being but did not create Himself but rather caused Himself to be. For Christians, in the beginning God created the heavens and the earth and all therein. The Qur'an corroborates that "Allah begets not, nor was He begotten" (sura 112, ayat 1-3). In Africa, too, God exists by Himself and was not created but known as the creator of all that were created.

Often, some Christians raise eyebrow when a fellow Christian exclaim 'Allah'. This is as a resullt of ignorance of the etymological concept of the word. As earlier cited in this book, Abd-Allah (20043) observed that:

> Etymologically, Allah comes from the same root as the Biblical words Elōhîm, ha-Elōhîm and hā-Elôh (all meaning God). Elōhîm derives from elôh (Hebrew for God), Alāhā is an emphatic form of alāh (Aramaic and Syriac for God) while Allah is connected to ilāh (Arabic for god).p.3.

Attributes of God

A closer examination of the attributes of God among known religions shows a very close relationship and leaves one to wonder why the constant religious crises that characterizes contemporary world. God is conceived in Islam as being absolutely One. In most, if not all religions, God is the creator of heaven, earth and underworld. Thus, Muslims know God as the Lord of the seven heavens and the Lord of the Great Throne.

God is the sustainer of all that were created. To God belong all the Most Beautiful Names in the world and despite these names, these religions believe that they are not sufficient to describe this mighty creator. He is most Gracious, Most Merciful, Omniscience, omnipresence, Supreme Judge and Protector and a host of other attributes. These attributes of God are the same in many known religions.

Myths of Origin

Islam teaches that Allah has no historical source. He is the only one who knows when He has been existing. He has no beginning and has no end. A philosophical expression in this respect states that "Allah is the First Cause, the only Cause and the Uncaused Cause (Ekeke & Ekeokpara, 2010). This agrees with the Qur'ān 57: 3 which says:

> He is the First (nothing is before Him) and the Last (nothing comes after Him) and Most High (nothing is above Him) and Most Near (nothing is nearer than He). And He is All-Knower of everything.

A similar expression is also witnessed in Christianity for example. In such religion, there is no myth associated with the origin of God. From the creation narration in the book of Genesis, the spirit of God was hovering over the face of the earth, implying that there is no record of his origin since God created all that were created. African Traditional Religion and other known religions also corroborrate this view.

Relationship between God and Man

Among known religions too, God is supreme and His sovereignty over man and the dependency of man on supersensible powers cannot be overemphasized. It is widely believed that the Supreme Being is invisible or inaccessible to humans. They believe that God, Allah, Supreme Being or any other name by which He is known is a spirit, who alone exists of himself and has no beginning or end. The Qur'an states that "Allah the self-Sufficient Master Whom all creatures need. And there is none co-equal or comparable to Him." (Sura 112, ayat 1-4). He is, therefore, above man and man has no option but to worship and plead for His favours and protection.

Chapter nine | Ezenweke, Elizabeth Onyedinma, in
Ezenweke, Elizabeth Onyedinma (Ed.)
Whose God Is God? Exploring The Concept Of God Within Religions
London & Abuja, Adonis & Abbey Pulishers

Subordinate

Many known religions hold that God is so pure that He needs not be contaminated by man. As such, He distanced Himself and created intermidiaries to associate with man. Some others, such as African Traditional Religion, profess that due to constant disturbances from man He delegated functions to intermidiaries for the day to day affairs of man. Still others, such as Chistianity and Judaism hold that the brightness or radiant light from God is so blazing that man needs intermidiaries to approach Him. In all these, intermidiaries were created by God as messengers and they derive powers and authorities from God. Thus, Christianity considers Christ as the son of God and Messiah, as well as a model to inspire all believers. After Jesus Christ, come other intermediaries like angels and saints while African Traditional Religions also believe in other subordinate gods.

In the notion of the new age movement, Bailey (1964) states that "God, greater than the created whole, yet God present also in the part; God transcendent guarantees the plan for our world and is the purpose, conditioning all lives from the minutest atom, up through all the kingdoms of nature to man" (p. 142).

However, Islam takes exception to the above view. In Islam, Allah has no associate to consult or receive assistance from. It has been noted in this work that to affiliate such to Allah is a grievous sin in the sight of Allah and a threat to Islamic Monotheism.

Summary

In summary, therefore, it has been observed that religion and religious issues have contributed immensely to known crises in human societies from the outset of history. This may be due to the fact that God, the essence of religion is understood and worshipped in various ways in various cultures. Moreso, religion itself is viewed from various perspectives. Notwithstanding the different shades of perspectives of religion as earlier pointed out, most known religions share some basic characteristics. Thus, in reality, the main essence is the same and so, God is God. Invariably, discord arising from the practice of religion or doctrinal matters may be rightly seen as fighting over the same coin with different shades. A good illustration of this same coin may be viewed from the perspectives of Judaism (traditional/indegenous religion), Christianity and Islam.

Judaism is the oldest Abrahamic religion which is a typified stance of the traditional religion of indegenous people. The adherents of Judaism (people of ancient Israel and Judea), believe that they are direct children of Abraham. Their primary source being the law, torah in Hebrew referring to the first five books of the Old Testament which is believed to have been handed over to them by God through Moses. Judaism gave birth to a set of twin brothers – Christianity and Islam. This is so because two of them sprang from the two sons of Abraham. Christianity is traced to the root of Isaac, the son of Sarah, while Islam is traced to the root of Ishmeal the son of Hagar. Christianity has Jesus Christ as the founder while Muhammed found Islam. Christianity, the second Abrahamic religion has the New Testament as its source while Islam, the third Abramic religion, has the quran and professes absolute monotheism.

A critical study of the Abramic religions as a good example of world religions and African traditional religion which is the indegenous and undiluted religion of Africans before it came into contact with external civilization reveals sufficient evidence to conclude that God is God in every religion.

Reference

Abd-Allah, U. F. (2004) *One God Many Names*. Nigeria: Nawawi Foundation.

Bailey, A.A. (1964). *Problems of Humanity*. New York: Lucis Trust.

Ekeke, E. C. & Ekeokpara, C. A. (2010). God, Divinities and Spirits in African Traditional Religious ontology in American Journal of Social and Management Sciences. http://www.scihub.org/AJSMS

Esptein, G. M. (2010). *Good Without God: What a Billion Nonreligious People Do Believe*. New York: HarperCollins.

Fitzgerald, T. (2000), *The Ideology of Religious Studies*. New York: Oxford University Press

Chapter nine	Ezenweke, Elizabeth Onyedinma, in Ezenweke, Elizabeth Onyedinma (Ed.) *Whose God Is God? Exploring The Concept Of God Within Religions* London & Abuja, Adonis & Abbey Pulishers

Prentiss. C. R. (2003). *Religion and the Creation of Race and Ethnicity.* New York: NYU Press.

Index

A

Anthropology, 5, 71, 73, 133, 138, 153
Atheists, 17, 25, 26, 27, 72, 107
ABDU-RAHEEM, M, 49
Achebe, Chinua, 142, 149
African language, 125
African myths, 127
African traditional religion, 15, 109, 126, 158
Al-Jannah, 55
Al-Quddūs, 56
Angels, 51, 62
Anya-na-ene-uwa, 129
Apostles' Creed, 45
Aquinas, Thomas, 19, 28, 29, 47, 83, 87, 90, 97, 98, 99, 100, 101, 102, 104, 105, 106
Augustinian Institute, 133

B

Bailey, Alice A, 67, 78
Believers, 6, 18, 51, 53, 63, 71, 106, 129
Bellah, Robert, 48
Berlin, 18
Brücke, Ernst, 20

C

Catechism, 30, 48
Cathedral, 88
Catholic, 27, 28, 30, 46, 48, 99, 108
Charismatic prophet s, 154
Constant equilibrium, 124

Contemporaneous Spiritualism, 74
Cosmic forces., 7
Charismatic individuals, 11
Chi, 118, 127, 128, 133, 134, 140, 141, 145, 146, 147, 149
Chineke, 118, 125, 127, 137
Christ College, 88
Christian Doctrine, 30
Christian funeral, 27
Christian Science, 70, 71, 72
Christianity, 13, 30, 31, 40, 43, 70, 72, 76, 84, 87, 100, 135, 150, 151, 155, 156, 157, 158
Christology, 134, 135, 136, 149, 150, 151
Church, 45, 48, 90, 91, 99
Contingency of Finite Beings, 102
Cosmological arguments, 87
Cosmologies, 109
Course in Miracles, 79, 85

D

Dabar, 31, 32, 45
Demons, 36, 135
Divine attributes, 57, 69
Divine pattern, 19
Divinely appointed leaders, 13
Divinity, 32, 50, 68, 69, 71, 76, 77, 78, 80, 83, 130, 131, 136, 148
Deity, 33, 47, 69, 70, 71, 72, 73, 75, 76, 79, 80, 82
Dewey, John, 31, 32, 39, 41, 42, 46, 47, 80, 84, 88, 99, 110, 135, 136
Divine Approaches, 69

Doctrinal matters, 157
Dominican order, 98
Dominicans, 99
Durkheim, Emile, 17

E

Eddy, Mary Baker, 70, 84
Elements of religion, 14
Egypt, 34, 35, 45, 137
El Elyon, 33
El Shaddai, 33
Elohim, 33
Ezenweke, Elizabeth, 7, 14, 15, 150

F

Feuerbach, Ludwig, 17, 28, 110
Father image, 21
Fufu, 127
Findhorn Foundation, 77, 78, 83
Freud, Sigmund, 17, 20, 21, 28

G

God's penetrating gaze, 19
Gödel, Kurt, 22

H

Halakha, 43
Hegelian philosophy, 18
Heidegger, Martin, 27
Holy Ghost, 44
Holy Spirit, 32, 44, 45, 74, 77
Hume, David, 89, 134, 135

I

I Am That I Am, 34, 38

Igbo-African, 133, 134, 138, 148
Infinite force, 39
Inherent divinity, 69
Interior spiritual man, 69
Indegenous religion, 158
Infinite Intelligence, 73
ISLAM, 49
Israel, 33, 34, 36, 37, 45, 46, 47, 48, 158

J

James, William, 22, 88, 91, 98, 149
Jesus Christ, 31, 32, 35, 40, 48, 50, 134, 136, 151, 155, 157, 158
Judaism, 30, 31, 33, 34, 39, 41, 42, 43, 47, 74, 87, 125, 157, 158
Judeo-Christian sphere, 81

K

Kant, Immanuel, 7, 15
Kanu, Ikechukwu Anthony, 17, 87, 133
Kardec, Allan, 74
King in His Majesty, 56
King of Salem, 33

L

Literary creativity, 19
Luis Santamaría, 67

M

Marx, Karl, 17, 18, 21, 27
Marxist atheism, 22
Medieval World', 23
Meketa, 118, 130
Mgbemena Stanley, 87
Monastery of Fossanuova, 99

Mulungu, 115, 116, 117, 120, 121, 122
Muslim, 15, 64, 66
Myths, 63, 85, 124, 156

N

Neopaganism, 75, 76, 83
New Age, 67, 71, 76, 77, 82, 83, 84, 85, 86
Northern Africa, 137
NSAC, 73
Nupe, 118, 127, 128

O

OGADA, CHARLES, 29
Old Testament, 31, 32, 33, 34, 39, 44, 45, 46, 48, 135
Omnipotent, 52, 72, 128
Omniscient, 61, 72
Ontological, 87, 89
Onwu, 141
Osanobua, 117, 127

P

Paris, 28, 98
Patristic period, 135
Paul, Jean, 17, 19, 28
Pharaoh, 52
Pontius Pilate, 42
Pope St. Pius V, 99
Panentheist philosophical systems, 82
Psychological account, 26
Pre-Christian Paganism, 75
Priestly Blessing, 43
Prophet Muhammad, 49, 50, 55, 59, 62, 64, 65, 66
Proslogion, 90, 94

Q

Qur'ān, 50, 51, 52, 53, 54, 55, 56, 59, 61, 63, 64, 156

R

Red Iberoamericana, 67
Radical relativism, 81
Roaring thunders, 124
Rule of Faith, 44

S

Saint Anselm, 90
Saint Augustine, 25
Schleiermacher, Friedrich, 17, 24
Scientific Atheism, 23
Second World War., 19
Self-Spirituality, 81
Slave morality, 24
Supernatural power, 124
Supernatural powers, 6
Supersensible forces, 7
Supreme Being, 155, 156
Supreme Intelligence, 74
Supreme Power, 72
Supreme Soul of the universe, 35
Supreme Being, 14, 50, 52, 69, 96, 117, 125, 126, 127, 137, 145, 146, 148, 153, 155
Sura, 155, 156

T

Tawḥīd, 51, 52, 53, 54
Teleological, 87, 88
Temple in Jerusalem, 38, 43
THANATOLOGY, 17
The Aquarian Conspiracy, 76, 84

The Council of Chalcedon, 136
The Messenger of Allah, 49
The Most High, 59
Theosophy legacy, 70
Tillich, Paul, 17, 19, 28, 43, 84, 85, 88
Trinitarian, 32, 44, 45, 70, 73
Telos, 87
Theologian class, 134
Transcendent being, 6
Transpersonal psychology, 83
Trinity, 50, 73
Tylor, E. B, 131

U

Uganda, 121, 122
Unity of Lordship, 52
Unity School, 72, 84
Unity School of Christianity, 72

Utilitarianism, 23
Umunna, 138, 142

W

Western Sahara, 137
Whitwell, Joseph P, 73

Y

Yahweh, 33, 34, 35, 36, 37, 43, 46, 47, 48, 125
YHWH, 31, 32, 33, 34, 35, 36, 37, 38, 39, 40, 41, 42, 43, 44, 45, 46, 47

Z

Zambia, 122, 123

www.ingramcontent.com/pod-product-compliance
Ingram Content Group UK Ltd.
Pitfield, Milton Keynes, MK11 3LW, UK
UKHW041259180426
11947UKWH00008B/567